PRAISE FOR *HOLY REBELLION*

"In a time when we desperately need alternatives to the performance and power that dominate so much of contemporary culture, the story of Christi Byerly's journey from religious abuse towards revolutionary love reveals the forces that are dividing our social fabric. This is a precious testimony that love, not righteousness, is the key to our humanity. A must-read for anyone seeking to understand the process of how good people get caught up in bad systems, and how we find our way out."
**– Clare Norman, Master Coach and Author of
*The Transformational Coach and Cultivating Coachability***

"This book brought me to tears. It reveals the quiet devastation of indoctrination, beliefs lived without question, where religion can eclipse curiosity and compassion. And yet, at its heart is Christi: a woman whose journey radiates love, joy, and deep acceptance of difference. Through her healing, old patterns are broken, generations are touched, and a powerful reminder emerges that reclaiming our humanity begins with choosing love."
– Debbie Brupbacher, Executive Transformation Coach

"Sometimes you cross paths with people who change the course of your existence. Through Awaken, Christi did just that – in her deeply human, spiritual, and loving way. I am beyond grateful for everything she's shared with me and wholeheartedly celebrate the publication of her debut memoir."
– Solène Anglaret, Consultant, Coach & Creative. Founder of Be Beyond Borders and author of five books, including travel memoir: *Where to Next?*

"*Holy Rebellion* is a homecoming for anyone who survived systems that called themselves loving and dared to question them. Christi writes for those shaped by religious abuse and family conditioning who carried both the cost of that harm and the deep, persistent knowing that love had to be more than this. With courage and compassion, this book helps untangle love from fear and faith from coercion. *Holy Rebellion* points beyond inherited beliefs and borrowed identities toward a Love vast enough to hold your questions, your grief, and your becoming. A Love that was never owned by any system and never stopped reaching for you."
– Valeyne Grotrian, Founder, Agora Coaching & Training Solutions

"I have been part of the Awaken Community for several years, and I have always been struck by Christi Byerly's deep and consistent purpose: creating communities of grace. Awaken itself is a living expression of that vision.

Reading her memoir, I finally understood where this calling was born. Christi's healing did not remain a private, personal journey; it became a collective one. She transformed the abuse she experienced within a religious system into a lifelong commitment to love, strength, and radical acceptance, embodying these values with courage and integrity.

Through her story and her lived purpose, Christi offers a message of profound hope to anyone who has been wounded by dysfunctional systems and is willing to go inward, uncover the truth, and rediscover the love that connects us all."
– Anna Moretti, founder of The Highly Sensitive Coach

"Christi is a hug for our soul and a nudge to our spirit in a time I believe our world deeply needs both. Creating communities of grace being her specialty, she empowers all she touches to live

out their unique divine assignment with self-alignment. Whoah, what a priceless gift Christi is to humanity. Through her work of Awaken Coach Institute, and her courageous exploration of her own journey on planet earth, may we be so grateful she shares herself and her learnings so candidly so we can all be more brave and loving listeners and light for each other."
– Lori Campbell

"Christi is evidence of the power of a self-coherent being to influence the environment. She creates waves of connection with her being."
– Deb Mohr, Becoming Mohr

"Christi came into my life when we joined forces to move diversity forward in the business agenda – volunteering, giving, that's her signature. Next, I dived into one of her many communities of love, Awaken Coach Institute; she was our master coach, sharing the right stories at the right times to bring abundance and possibilities into our lives. Now, she brings all those stories and more to us as a gift. With her heart open, she offers lines that shine a light in the lives of those who read these pages with a heart wide open."
– Eduardo dos Santos Silva, Technology Executive, Leadership Coach and author of *A Life in Motion*

"Christi weaves words with tenderness born from lived experience. Through deep personal work, she transforms trauma into a language of acceptance and hope, offering readers a compassionate companion on their own healing journey."
– Stacy Crawford, Founder of Klear Water Coaching & Wellness LLC

HOLY REBELLION

Holy Rebellion: Waking up from Religious Abuse

Published by TWH Press in the United Kingdom 2026

Paperback ISBN: 978-1-918485-02-8
eBook ISBN: 978-1-918485-03-5

Publishing partnership with TWH Press
twhpress.com

Cover design by Christine Goldschmidt
Instagram: @christinegoldschmidt_1

Typesetting by The Book Typesetters
thebooktypesetters.com

HOLY REBELLION

Waking up from Religious Abuse

Christi Byerly

CONTENTS

FOREWORD

My husband and I first connected with Christi through hosting her Awaken Coach Institute training retreats each year at our retreat center in Spain on the pilgrimage route to Santiago de Compostela. As our friendship and working relationship developed, I participated in one of her training retreats myself, and we also began offering some of our own retreat experiences for her groups.

One of these activities is building and walking a labyrinth together, which we both share a deep love for. I love that Christi has weaved the labyrinth symbol into her book.

The labyrinth is beautiful because it is a living symbol, layered with meaning. Each person has their own experience of it and their own way of walking. At its core, the labyrinth is an archetype of pilgrimage—a symbol of the life journey of healing, transformation and maturation. In some of the oldest known labyrinths, we can see that the labyrinth is born from a circle and a square (or an equidistant cross), and this pattern appears again and again across traditions.

The circle represents the circular journey: we leave home, we walk the path, and we return, hopefully transformed in some way. It speaks of dusk and dawn, death and rebirth—life's great rhythm of continually being stretched out of the old and into the ever-new spaces and horizons that life nudges us towards. The labyrinth journey is a journey of courage, especially for those who have no choice but to walk it and heal. Such a journey can break you open into the deeper mysteries of love.

The square, or equidistant cross, at the center of a labyrinth points to a "four-ness." Anthropologists, mythologists, psychologists and nature itself return to this structure as a map for transformation. How do we continually face change? How do we move through liminality, challenge and difficulty? How do we receive gifts, joy and boons along the way? And most importantly, how do we carry it back into the world—into community, into relationships—not as something we hold only privately but as something that becomes an offering? How do we mature in service?

I am grateful to have read Christi's book, as it helped me understand what has formed such a remarkable woman. Every part of her brave journey has shaped her, and she has transformed that journey into service—guiding others with openness, humor, integrity, compassion and an embodied wisdom that can only come from someone who has truly walked the walk.

What I have witnessed over the years is her courage to be real and vulnerable, her strength, tenderness, humor and humility. She is not interested in power, but in people. In nurturing them, training them, seeing the gifts in them, and exquisitely encouraging them to rise into their potential. Through this generosity, she has built through Awaken not only a program, but a living community—a community of beloveds.

I recommend this book to anyone who is standing at a threshold in their life, feeling the call to change, or seeking a deeper understanding of their own journey. It is especially powerful for those drawn to pilgrimage, inner work, coaching, or soul-led transformation.

Some books don't simply tell a story—they carry a path.

Basia Goodwin, co-owner of the *Flores del Camino* retreat center

Basia's Blessing:

*May this book find the right hands at the right time,
and gently guide its reader home to their own story.*

ENTERING THE LABYRINTH

As I write, I keep labyrinths all around—a pewter Chartres labyrinth in a red pouch with a stylus, a wooden finger labyrinth, and a labyrinth drawn on paper with markers. It's my favorite way to meditate and brings back a world of memories.

My first time walking a labyrinth is in Kenya at the base of the Ngong Hills. I am at Mwangaza Jesuit retreat center, and the labyrinth is made of brick hidden in the grass under an enormous blessing tree. I am there on an eight-day silent retreat, and my one break from the silence is a short meeting each morning with Sister Pat.

I'm with the Jesuits because, at nearly 40, my world has been turned upside down by the coach training I am undertaking. Everything I thought was true now feels false. Those thoughts tumble through my body in confusion.

I'm not Catholic, but I hope that the Catholics will bring me back to some enduring, timeless, solid faith. Sister Pat is a spunky, beautifully yet soberly dressed nun who walks me through an Ignatian-based spiritual retreat. For all I know, it might be heretical, but it seems solidly grounded in scripture, so I'm not too worried.

Ignatian spiritual retreats are divided into four sections, corresponding to the stages of the spiritual journey. Each section is called a "Week," and an Ignatian retreat can take thirty days to complete or even a whole year in everyday life. An eight-day retreat to complete all four Weeks is on the speedy side, but it's more than long enough for me, as all those days in silence are daunting.

Week one is about God's love and mercy. First is the hidden life of Christ—that period where he's a child growing in wisdom and stature. Little is known about that time, except that his parents believe he is the Son of God and are raising him in love.

Week two takes the retreatant into the leadership of Christ as he becomes an adult and performs miracles. In Week three, we follow Christ into his suffering and death as he takes on the sins of the world. And in Week four, we experience resurrection and mission in a glorious finale.

It's new, and I am excited to start, especially the parts about leadership, suffering, and glory. Bring it on!

However, Sister Pat guides me to Bible passages about love. It's almost sickly sweet. There are lilies of the field. There are sheep safely grazing. There is artwork, music, and the scents of cloying essential oils to be contemplated silently and journaled upon. I quickly realize it's designed to soften me into a lovey-dovey childlike state.

In days three and four, we're meant to move on to teachings about leadership, which I feel ready for. At this stage in my life, leadership should be happening. I'm in my prime, and I've had a stellar career trajectory. I've been known as the "rising star" and the "stealth bomber" in my high-powered lobbying and press relations job in nuclear energy, culminating in an enviable move to Paris. But Sister Pat keeps offering me verses about love, flowers, birds, and the like.

After studying the leadership verses, we are meant to contemplate sin and suffering. I'm a sin aficionado, having been raised on it. That's my wheelhouse. But, as days five and six roll on, we're still namby-pambying with verses on love, peace, joy, kindness, goodness, yada-yada-yada. As the retreat closes, with the final two days meant to be about resurrection, I'm still playing with the kiddie verses about love.

Annoyed, I ask Sister Pat why we never bothered to follow the retreat script, as everyone else had. She says, "There's no point going on a spiritual journey until you know you're loved. You haven't received the grace yet, so I can hardly have you look at leadership or sin, can I? It would be too much." I leave the retreat disappointed, but she offers to meet with me monthly as a follow-up.

I continue to meet her without fail every month for the next five years. It's not until three years later that she introduces me to different kinds of verses—ones filled with power and darkness.

I notice the difference, and Sister Pat tenderly lets me know she can see I know a little of love. I'm amazed she stuck with me for three years, never moving on from love, love, and more love. It's humbling to have taken so long to "get it." Each month, I've come with stories of self-blame and self-condemnation, and each month she reminds me I'm loved.

Throughout those years together, Sister Pat sends me out, month after month, to walk the labyrinth at the Mwangaza retreat center. Its patterns are etched in my soul, and I feel its mysteries in my bones. This labyrinth follows a simplified version of the seven-circuit Chartres pattern.

When you walk a labyrinth, most people take a deep breath before setting an intention for the journey—by asking a question or inviting awareness of a topic. I never have a clue what my intention is; I just hope the path will have its own. Then, you take your first step, due east, into the entrance. You're facing the center, so you have some idea there's a destination. In fact, it's right in front of you and not too far.

The next thing you know, you've taken a sharp left turn and, quickly, you're confused because you don't know how far you've walked. You keep walking, with so many meanders, as they're called. You've gone a long way, and then after you've walked for half an hour, you discover you're nearly back where you started, swooped as far from center as ever. You wonder why this journey is so long, and where it's going. What's the goal?

If others are walking the labyrinth, your paths cross. You're walking right, they're walking left, and it's impossible to know whether they are walking toward the center or walking in the opposite direction. Just because you look like you're walking in opposite directions doesn't mean you are—you're all on the same path.

And nobody on the path judges you. You could sit and wail at a particular bend. You can stand, squat, or lie prostrate in the center. You can decorate the labyrinth with your tears, or roses or stones. If fifty people walk a labyrinth, it'll be adorned with roses in many places, each turn holding its unique gestalt.

As you walk, you keep coming to places where you have to do an about-face. Sometimes it's only a quarter of the way around, and you do a little back and forth, back and forth weave. In other parts, you're walking all the way around the edge a long time, and then, you're turning in the complete opposite direction. Just when you're at your most confused, and halfway in, halfway out because you've been turned around so often, there is one last little journey, and you're dumped into the center somewhat unceremoniously.

Ouf! There you are in the giant, pulsing heart of the labyrinth, and there is an emotional release. Everything comes to a standstill. There's nothing. There's everything. There's death. Eventually, there's life. Sometimes, a person will have placed literal dry bones in the center. You meet the mythic Minotaur.

You can stay as long as you like, just being. Nothing has to happen. The stories, narratives, roles, and identities made up by culture and context fade. You can feel your lungs expand, an eternal power pumping through your heart. This is where you reflect on the journey so far, a resting point. It's also a time to face mortality. You feel you've come a long way; the most challenging part is over. You might even feel you've arrived. But the journey is only half complete.

Then you just stand up and begin the journey outward. It

reminds me of taking a shower when, without prompting, you turn the water off and decide it's over.

That journey outward is different; you know more about what to expect. You know how long the journey takes. You have seen each circuit, each meander. What felt so true, so important, and stressful at this or that turn on the way in, has a different perspective, a lightness, a truth.

You have walked it all before, but you are no longer heading into yourself anymore. It is not that sort of contemplative, moving-toward-darkness journey. You have passed the darkness that comes before dawn. It's more confident because of the learning and power you feel from having met your inner angels and demons in the labyrinth's center, and your own ephemeral nature.

As you are walking out, you may still meet people, but in a more solid, grounded way. Like when you go on a long hike, and have reached the summit and are coming back down, and you murmur encouragement to those still climbing the slopes. In the hero's journey, it's coming home and the outward journey is different. This time, as you go through the twists and turns and see people walking in different directions, there's less confusion and more steadiness, and you can see people through the bigger picture.

Again, the end comes unexpectedly. You are dumped back out into the world after seemingly endless looping. You arrive where you started. But you are different.

Leadership is now a given—because you know yourself as the ruler of your kingdom. Out there in the wide world, your real journey begins. You may have had a wonderful spiritual experience walking the labyrinth, but you're still going to meet people who don't know you've changed, or who hold to the old stories they created about you before you started.

So, when you get dumped back out, there is a moment where

you take another deep breath and realize who you've become. You're living your life differently, and you're going to need to retrain a few people to know who you are now.

A labyrinth isn't a maze, as you're never lost. There's only one path. And the goal is not a destination; it's about returning to what seems like the exact same spot. You've come into true power. Once again, back in the world of systems, roles, religions, capitalism, success, and achievement, it all feels different.

When you're walking, it isn't clear, but then when you rise above, each turn is purposeful, planned, and gorgeous. When you look down on a labyrinth, it's obvious the whole thing is built of beautiful patterns and flow. There's a regular rhythm. The plot doesn't make sense without each turn happening exactly the way it did, both the journey in and the journey out.

This book is the labyrinthine story of my life, and the circuits and meanders that changed me. Its three-part structure of the meanderings, center and return hold the stories that contain my confusions, miseries, and despair. But also, moments of dramatic truths, ever-so-slow learning from what I didn't do as much as what I did, and the joy, power, and energy of knowing myself as the ruler of my lands.

It brings me to this day, when I still forget I'm infinitely valuable, just like you are. When I still panic that my dearest ones won't love me anymore. When I still forget that none of us gets to lead, take on the struggles of the world, or rise victorious unless we can come back to love again and again.

In Greek artwork, the "meander" is a common ornamentation, with many patterns. A false meander continues in a spiral, without making an about-face. But a true meander must include a complete change of direction. Its lines turn first inwardly and then outwardly. The true meander is the type used in labyrinths to reach the center, and return to the outside world.

In my evangelical childhood, we were taught to "repent" or turn from our sin and toward righteousness. As an adult, I learned to repent of this stilted righteousness, and turn toward being fully alive, awake, messy, and joyful. The truth, confusingly, was the opposite of all I was taught. This book is filled with my memories of both these times and reflects my personal experiences and recollections.

Along this journey, the names and identifying characteristics of some individuals have been altered to protect their privacy. I've written two of our children's names and genders in neutral form, with they/them pronouns. While I have done my best to offer a story as true as memory allows, I acknowledge memory is subjective and imperfect, and others may recall events differently.

There is so much innocence and beauty in the world. And so much darkness and violence. We see this especially dramatically in systems that try to pretend they're good, exclusive, or better than others. These cult-like systems can feel all-encompassing, but there is an off-ramp. It is possible to exit them and find a world of love and acceptance.

If you have been told who you are and where you belong all your life, you can feel completely devoid of identity without the system you are now obliged to uphold. The more we try to idealize ourselves, the more darkness we must hide, which is a dangerous dynamic. The more we can accept our humanity, the better we are able to behave.

This book is for you if you want to know deep in your bones that you're completely loved, and that it couldn't possibly be otherwise. And that you're the undisputable ruler of your kingdom. You get to choose your community, companions and who you champion.

That's true even if, like me, you've been told you're anything less than lovable, less than deserving. That you're defective in some way. That your thoughts and feelings don't matter.

I'm here to tell you that couldn't possibly be true. You will find love outside of the system you're in. Your true nature is Love. Period. And Love will stick with you until you know it.

WALK YOUR OWN LABYRINTH

To walk a labyrinth is a quiet, yet revolutionary act. It's so different from standing on the edges, watching someone else walk it. Once you step in, and you're putting one foot in front of the other, you're entering into rhythm. You're surrendering to a timeless moving meditation.

It is the refusal to take the shortest distance between two points, opting instead for the sacred detour. The path is not a puzzle to be solved, but a surrender to be lived. It reminds you that in the divine geometry of your life, you are never lost, even as the path turns on itself.

I created The Awaken Way as an open invitation as you find yourself longing to walk your own labyrinth journey. I'm offering you this four-lesson experience because I want you to access the epic pattern: the inward journey, the center, and the return.

In this course, I've poured some of the deepest gems I've learned from my own journey as a coach, as a leader, and as a mother. We're all walking each other home, and my hope is that these four lessons will be a trustworthy companion on the path.

As you move through the course, I invite you to expand time. Though it may only take you a couple of hours to complete, when you slow down and savor those moments, you may discover what took me years to learn:

Love itself has been holding you all along.

The Path is trustworthy.

And you're ready now, not because you've "arrived," but because transformation happens as you walk.

You can visit *awakencoachinstitute.com/the-awaken-way* to begin.

In the Great Love, **Christi**

LOVE REBEL

*"You do not have to walk on your knees for a hundred miles
through the desert repenting."*
Mary Oliver

I'm 17 years old. My hand is on the doorknob of Dr. Stevenson's office at college. I'm about to have a conversation that will end in me being expelled. My life is about to be ruined.

To understand the stakes, you'd need to know that I was raised in the kind of utopian/dystopian household that featured in the documentary *Shiny, Happy People*. It was a home in which punishment was swift and early, and rewards meted out based on accomplishment and upholding the "model Christian" image of my family.

Such was my belief and fear in my identity as a sinner that when I was 12, and six years younger than most, I chose to Profess my Faith in front of my church. This entailed memorizing the Heidelberg Catechism, an oral exam on a series of fifty-two weeks of questions centered around the concepts of Guilt, Grace, and Gratitude. If I passed, I would stand before the congregation to sign on to a life of gratitude—appreciative that I would not burn in hell despite my utter depravity.

Most people in my church community went through the process in a rote fashion, as a group at age 18. But I was much too scared of burning in hell for all eternity to wait that long. I needed to profess early to bring myself some relief from my fear.

So, as a skinny 12-year-old girl, I faced an all-male group of church leaders, responding to such questions as, "What is your only comfort in life and in death?" with answers such as, "That I am not my own, but belong body and soul to my Lord and Savior Jesus Christ."

The elders of the church asked why I wanted to profess so young, and I responded with an impassioned speech about the depth of my sinful nature and longing for heaven, which they found quite impressive. It never crossed my mind that anyone on earth could believe otherwise, as my life consisted of home, church, and Christian school, where parents, students, and teachers alike signaled their commitment to the concept of the "Total Depravity of Man."

I rebelled ever so slightly at age 16, by choosing to go to a conservative Christian college that was considered liberal in my community, compared to the college where the members of my school and church were expected to attend. I was already so different from the others in my graduating class. They were all 18, and none carried their family's expectation that they become the class valedictorian.

Upon arrival at my new college, step one was to sign "The Pledge"—a document that committed me to a standard of acceptable behavior, which included no drinking alcohol, no smoking, no sex, and no (gasp) dancing, all of which were in line with my previous commitments. I happily signed on, and happily judged others who were expelled or suspended for recklessly abandoning their God-ordained commitments to pure living. You smoked? Suspended. Simple.

Except it is now me who has broken the rules.

I knock on the door and only turn the doorknob when I hear Dr. Stevenson's call to enter. He greets me with a smile and asks about my trip to France for the French language summer program. He had taken a risk sending me; I was three years younger than my peers, but I had nowhere to go over the summer holidays. The previous Christmas, my total depravity had been too much for my mother. I must have rolled my eyes too many times, or not done my share of the dishes, because she forbade me from coming home during my summer break, saying she'd probably kill me if she had to spend more than two weeks at a time with me under the same roof. Dr. Stevenson took pity, found a loophole, and sent me to France. I had repaid him by ensuring his first job of the new semester was expelling me.

"How was your host family?" he asks.

He does not yet touch on the fact that while I was away, I had forgotten to attend classes and cultural outings and consequently received failing D minus grades on all ten credit hours. I was done for. When I arrived back at college for the fall semester, I received my report card, and it showed that I had earned all A minus grades—nearly the top scores. I couldn't believe my summer French teachers would have ever done such a thing, so there had to have been a mistake. I was flunking out of school, and more depraved than ever.

With a deep trembling in my stomach, I explain that my host family had been kind and generous, but the woman I was staying with had been called away and left me with her 19-year-old son. Dr. Stevenson frowns, and I hurriedly explain that the son was charming and the perfect gentleman. I, however, when left unchaperoned, was not the perfect Christian.

I've been trained to confess my sins and take the punishment for my faults, so I'm ready to confess. I bow my head and begin.

"We went to Madonna and Midnight Oil concerts as

bartenders, serving beer to the crowds. We went to neighbors' pool parties until 4 a.m. We sipped wine and champagne under the plane trees on the Avignon center square. We went to topless beaches—" Dr. Stevenson stands and quickly crosses the room to close his office door. "I smoked my first cigarette. I broke nearly every rule in 'The Pledge' and with the greatest enthusiasm—even dancing!"

I am too embarrassed to add there had been no sex because I was one hundred percent convinced of immediate punishment by disease or pregnancy.

His reply floors me, "No wonder you speak such great French! You lived the real French experience, which you never would have gotten in a classroom. We're going to make a deal. Sometimes the rules are made to be broken. You must *never* tell anyone here this story before you graduate, or your grades go back to D minus. As long as this stays between us, I'm going to keep your grades as an A minus. You're a great student, and I'm proud of you for being brave enough to have some fun."

I am stunned. He is the Bishop of Digne to my Jean Valjean. My life is not over, because he has chosen to give it back to me.

In that moment, I understand guilt, grace, and gratitude in a profound, new way. I've been taught that life is about being good, a model student and Christian and following the rules. The law is about reward and punishment in accordance with sin.

Now I see a different truth. Life is about the pure joy of being alive and being loved. About listening deeply and treating others with kindness and compassion.

That moment is the beginning of my life of Holy Rebellion.

It's part of a much more ancient and universal tale. It leads me to want to see and love people for the beautiful, wonderful humans that they are—even and especially when they believe themselves to be wrong, small, sinful, or defiant.

Just as I had been trained to believe since birth.

PART ONE

THE MEANDERS

CHAPTER 1

AN INKLING OF THE TRUTH

"May we raise children who love the unloved things."
Nicolette Sowder

The grass is thick and damp under my toes. My tricycle lies on its side by the sidewalk. I'm not quite big enough to ride it alone. I'm vibrantly alive, with specks of apple on my chin. Stretching my arms high, I fling my apple core across the lawn and double over with laughter.

The world is enormous around me, and my little apple core lies where I tossed it, as I tumble into the leaves, sweet and rotting. I breathe in the scent of late August in New England.

"You pick up that apple core, young lady," my mom says, her voice clipped and strident. She's enormous, nearly six feet, and a force of energy.

I shake my head and stand to face her, clutching my fists tightly at my sides. "No!"

The apple core belongs out here. The ground is where apples go when they're done, and I'm meant to be playing. The lawn itself knows. But she doesn't.

She strides towards me, yanks my arm. My shoulder is tugged forward with a jolt, and my body with it. Her hand grasps mine, and she marches across the yard to the apple core. She will win this fight. But so will I.

"Pick it up."

My hand stays tightly wound into a fist. I am determined to outlast her. She pries open each finger and smashes my palm onto the cool, moist apple core. When my hand touches it, instinctively, it splays out fully extended, convex.

Now she must bend my fingers one by one around the apple core and keep her hand firmly around mine so I can't open it again. I've got a fist full of apple and grass.

She marches me across the lawn, up the front steps, and across the kitchen threshold. My bare feet skid across the cool linoleum floors. I'm leaning back, so she has to push me along. She plants me in front of the wastebasket, like it's an altar to obedience. I plant myself in front of it like it's an altar to my freedom.

"Open your hand."

I clench tighter. My tiny fingers curl around that disintegrating apple core, refusing to lose this battle. I grip it so tightly I could squeeze the core out of existence. My jaw locks. I feel my body tremble with the fire of defiance.

She pries at my fingers, one by one, until they finally open over the wastebasket. The apple core drops, sounding hollow against the metal can. My sticky hand is empty. She exhales, victorious, her shoulders straightening in confirmation of her role as a "good mother."

Inside me, something hardens. I know myself as far more powerful than she. The force of my loathing will keep me alive.

More than a decade later, I'm finishing my day at my high school where my mom also works. I dread the days I stay late in the library, shelving books or organizing cards alphabetically, wondering if my mom would have given one of my classmates an after-school detention. Wondering if those classmates would look at me spitefully from the tables where they were serving their time.

On a quiet Wednesday, I escape to the Spanish teacher's classroom, where a warm, peaceful atmosphere fills the space. I find a desk in the back to draw quietly, while Mrs. Martínez sits at her desk grading papers. My hair falling in front of my face, I surreptitiously observe her, soaking in the calm.

Her son is toddling around the classroom, exploring. Reaching tall, he can just manage to lift the lids on the desks and fiddle with the pencils in their ledges inside. He climbs up on the seats and observes what the high schoolers have left atop the smooth surfaces.

My heart is pounding for him. I am sure he will be hit, and I'm ready to spring to his rescue. He is touching things that don't belong to him. He is not asking permission. Surely, he must be a troublemaker, disturbing his mom's peace. I breathe shallowly, alert to defend him.

I glance at his mother. She sits at her desk, continuing with her work. From time to time, she stops to gaze tenderly at her darling child. Her eyes sparkle, her face soft. He looks up at her from time to time, content. Her dimpled smile shows all her slightly crooked ivories. She doesn't even try to keep from beaming.

"Isn't he so cute?" she says softly and warmly to me. "He's learning more every day."

My heart nearly breaks in two with longing. So that's what it would be like to explore freely and safely. That's what it's like to have love and trust between a mom and a toddler.

I tuck everything away for later—the glances, the smiles, the way it feels in that classroom. I know this is how it's meant to be. This could be normal.

My first week at college in September 1988, I'm registered for a speech class with only seven other students, and we're beginning with poetry. I'm standing at the center of the circle in a Ghanaian dress my brother has sent me from his year abroad, its blue batik fabric bright against the beige walls. I'm barefoot and playful as I leap about, animatedly reciting "Sensemayá," a rhythmic chant by a Cuban poet for killing a snake. I notice a tall, nerdy guy whose bright red hair catches the light from the window. He's gazing steadily at me and comes up to me after class to introduce himself and inquire where I got my dress.

Ben wears high-waisted brown pants that sit well above the hips, secured with a flat metal hook-and-bar fastener, and no pleats. His shirt is a button-down blue cotton, and he's got on ancient, scuffed dress shoes. Every other guy on campus wears relaxed stone-washed jeans, sneakers, and a t-shirt. His hair is neatly parted far to one side, and it's been slicked back as though with a wet comb. His pale skin is wizened and wrinkled, like he's spent most of his life on the equator.

He's the most attentive person I've ever met. He's really listening. As we walk across campus together, we compare schedules and laugh when we realize we share four courses, so we'll be spending most of our class time together.

Some classes are in cavernous lecture halls with rows of students. We slip into the back and pass notes. Little drawings, jokes about the professors, scraps of thought. Between classes, we meet in the cafeteria, trays balanced and find seats away from the hubbub.

With Ben, I don't have to perform. Given his attire, he clearly doesn't care what anyone thinks. I decide I don't have to impress. Sitting across from him feels easy. He's curious about everything, quick to smile. He's got a truly radiant smile with perfectly aligned teeth, and I find myself talking more freely than usual. Whenever we see one another, we always find seats together.

He's fascinating, and his stories take a long time to tease out, as he continually turns the conversation back to me. I do love to talk if anyone's willing to listen, so that suits me fine. He hides many things about himself. To some, he's from North Carolina. To others, he's grown up in Côte d'Ivoire. The truth is he spent one year at high school in the United States, when his parents were furloughed to America from their work as Bible school missionaries, before heading back to boarding school in West Africa. He chooses his stories based on the perceived interest level of his listeners. He charts his own course, not belonging to any one group, but easily conversing with everyone.

I find him fun and also mysterious. We don't date. Sometimes I need to line up to talk with him, as there are usually two or three other girls waiting to catch his ear. He's got a serious girlfriend from high school, so he's not available. Plus, I'm spending my time making sure no one mistakes me for a nerd, so I casually date a series of guys from the swim team, the football team, and our "brother dorm."

On a Saturday night in our senior year, my friends and I join a crowded house party off campus. Music thumps through the walls, and everyone's talking over each other, red plastic cups in every hand. I'm in a tight circle of six people, each of us laughing and shouting to be heard, as we wave our drinks overhead.

I notice Ben, leaning in the kitchen doorway, in his usual observer stance. His bright blue eyes take in everything. Someone bumps into my friend's arm, and her drink spills over, Diet Coke spreading across the floor. We all laugh and keep talking, helplessly wondering how we'll clean it up. None of us have napkins. Before I can take a step toward the kitchen, Ben is already crouching with a pair of thick dishcloths. No fuss, no announcement. He quietly blots up the spill, careful, methodical, and heads back to the kitchen.

It's such a small thing, but I feel it hit me hard, the way he notices what needs doing and does it without fanfare. Indiscriminately kind to everyone. This is the kind of steady person to hold on to. My chest tightens, my breath catches. In the middle of the noise and chaos, I realize I'm in love with him.

The next day, I'm having lunch with my friend Tracy. Her parents are marriage counselors in Alsace, France, and she is the dating expert. She grew up in France and has French handwriting, mannerisms, and a vivacious French party girl disposition. We've got a lot of classes together, because we're both getting double majors in French and communications, so we often find ourselves together. She's sexy and petite, with curly hair always styled with effortless elegance up in a clip. I feel like an oaf around her, but she teaches me how to clip my straight hair, too.

She says to me, "How come you've never dated Ben? You know, whenever we talk, it's always, 'Oh, Ben said this, and Ben did that.' I think you really like him!" I mildly protest, saying we have nothing in common. He's friends with all the missionary kids, wears free clothes from the missionary barrel, and is studying Bible. I hang out with the party people. But I secretly know she's right. I really do like him.

She insists, "I dare you to ask him out. You know TWIRP weekend is coming up. Perfect time to just 'twirp' him. You don't have to wait for the guy to make all the moves!"

TWIRP is our college's version of a Sadie Hawkins event, and stands for The Women Initiate Romantic Pursuits. A Christian college like ours is made for serious matchmaking followed by marriage. There are rules about dating, and people take it seriously. Yet, Tracy's being playful.

I decide, why not? It's senior year, we've been friends a long time, and what's the worst that can happen?

Finding him to ask him out is not a problem. We're next-door neighbors, each living in a house just off campus. Neither of us has signed up for the cafeteria meal plan this year because we're both super frugal. So, we need to shop at the local Safeway and cook for ourselves. I don't have a car, so when I need to go to the store, I regularly lie in wait for Ben to leave his house on his motorcycle.

It's a chilly January Tuesday when, from my living room window, I see him in his leather jacket buckling his helmet and getting ready to toss a leg over the wide, black frame of his Honda CX 500. I seize my jacket and head outside, waving him over. He grabs a second helmet, and I jump on behind him on the worn leather seat. He gives the engine a quick rev, and it takes off humming steadily. It's a practical, non-flashy bike, but we both think it's pretty cool. I like to look serene, but when he catches some air flying over the railroad tracks, I give a little scream and grab onto his waist.

We linger in the grocery store. I buy a rotisserie chicken, and he buys vegetables. I suggest we might as well team up and cook them together. Less work for us both.

After we put the food in his fridge, I casually ask, "So, what are you up to this weekend?"

"Oh, I have a missionary kid snow weekend in Michigan. We're all going tubing, and I'm driving the van. We'll be gone all weekend."

Even more casually, I slip in before leaving his house, "Oh, that's too bad. If you were here, I was going to TWIRP you. See you later!"

I discover two weeks later that this seemingly offhand remark has a serious impact. Ben calls his guy friends together to talk about what is to be done. He tells them he's had his eye on a few girls, most notably a traditional southern girl with big hair from Alabama, who would make a charming wife. But I'm fun, too, if not the kind of person he would have expected to date. But now, I've told him I would have TWIRPed him! Once I found out he'd be out of town, why did I still ask? It must be serious.

To him, I'm a "Wow" kind of girl, who's smart, funny, and going places. He could see it being an interesting relationship, but we're such good friends, and he wouldn't want to wreck anything. His guy friends encourage him to go for it and see what happens. But his younger sister, who's a year behind us and holds responsibility for his monthly home-style haircuts, is skeptical and protective. "Christi's a giant flirt! She's dated half the campus. She's not serious. You might get your heart broken. Go ahead and date if you want, just don't get the cart before the horse."

After more prayer, he decides to ask if I'll go with him to a mission's fundraising dinner the next Sunday night in the dining hall, which I don't think is a date. Usually, a couple of hundred people gather for worship songs, prayer, and sharing life stories in small groups. I agree, and we walk from our houses across campus, enjoying the dinner and singing, but skipping out before the speaker. When we get back to mine, instead of heading next door, he comes inside. My little sister Kathryn and her boyfriend are with us. We light a fire in the fireplace, make tea, and sit on the floor, comfortably laughing and talking.

After a while, Ben gets sleepy and sprawls on the couch. I sit on the couch in front of him. Kathryn's sleepy and is making moves to go home, when Ben gently strokes my back. *What is happening here?* I wonder. My sister wonders, too, and stays for a couple more hours, waiting for him to go home so she can ask me, "Are you guys dating?" Ben outlasts her, though, and leaves after her, with me no more clued in.

The next day, I can't stand the suspense any longer, so I make my way to Ben's house to ask him, "What's the deal?" He's a good friend, and we're graduating in just a few months. So, this is hardly the time to begin a harmless fling. He assures me he's made no lifelong decisions about us but figures we could get to know each other in a new way. If it works out, fantastic! And if not, well, that would be a "sad too bad."

I arrive in Kenya at the Jomo Kenyatta International Airport in a stupor, with two very sleepy children in tow. Leaving Paris after a severe burnout with no job ahead of me, I am looking forward to "deep rest," which is the opposite and the antidote to its homonym "depressed."

My husband, Ben, who arrived in Kenya two weeks before us, comes to the airport with my mom and dad. We have decided to get over jetlag at my parents' house for a couple of days, before bringing our kids, who are almost 5 and 2, into their dramatically different new environment. My mom wraps me in a big hug, and hands me a Nokia cell phone with phone credit already loaded, and both of their phone numbers saved.

My dad gives me an awkward squeeze and looks at me intently because my body is visibly shaking. I feel like I have arrived on unfamiliar shores after combat, and I can hardly keep upright. We hand our suitcases to a Kenyan man who has come with an extra car for our things. But one of our suitcases is lost, and I am the only one authorized to go back into the airport to fill out the lost luggage report. I'm not sure I can. I am near tears, and my muscles are failing me.

Confused, my dad says, "It's not that hard. You just fill out a form. Do you need me to go in with you?"

I shake my head, take a deep breath, and head back into the hot crowds in the airport, hoping my legs won't give before I finish standing in the chaotic queue. The job done, I sink into the back seat and lean into Ben. We're on a kamikaze slalom tour of the airport exit, swerving and bobbing to miss the bicycles, donkey carts, pedestrians, and yellow-striped *matatus* which are the local fourteen-seater buses.

Back in Ben's arms, I fall into a deep slumber, and we enjoy a couple of welcome days' rest at my parents' house. Refreshed, we head to the university campus where Ben has forty-eight months to complete a doctorate. We're about to meet our lodgings for the next four years.

I had written to Ben in advance. The faucets in our apartment sink are divided into hot and cold. I had told him that he needs to have the sink changed out so that the hot and cold will mix, lest one of our toddlers burn themselves on the water from the hot spout. He doesn't respond directly, just tells me I'll have time to get acclimated to everything when I arrive. I use the bathroom for the first time, turn on the hot water, and discover both the hot and cold taps produce lukewarm water. The shower is the same. Problem solved!

We're flooded with immediate friends and community. Our neighbors across the hall are eager to offer advice about hiring help, where to find food on campus, who to give money to, and more importantly, who not to help and who not to give money to. Their sweet and spunky daughter becomes fast friends with our little Micah.

On Leila's second birthday she's overwhelmed by hundreds of children staring at her, touching her pale, white face and reaching out for her wisps of blond hair. She's never been one to cling to her mom, but she does now. She leans away from the crowds and snuggles her head in my neck. We eat a dry and crumbling cake, make piles of popcorn, and do face painting for more than seventy-five kids who line up for the fun.

I'm still overwhelmed by the new sights and sounds. I'm slowly getting used to cooking on two burners from a blue gas bomb, like the ones an American might bring on camping trips.

There are only two drawers in the kitchen, from which cock-roaches scamper out at night. My neighbor, Mariam, from Burkina Faso in West Africa, shows up several nights during our first week with a delicious and beautifully arranged platter of crudités and a dish of meat. She helps me organize our things and sweep the floor. Then she offers to have her house helper come work for me part-time. Within days I can see that house help is not negotiable. There's no way one person can hand-wash all the clothes, hang them on the lines, fold them, cook all the meals from scratch, and watch toddlers.

A week later, I walk across campus to the cafeteria and see a willowy white woman with sleek, long hair, just older than me, wearing gorgeously draped designer attire. Her name is Florine, and I discover she's a licensed counselor working with a local counseling team, and her husband does IT work on campus, so she's our neighbor, too. I'm excited to know that there's a coun-selor available and tell her I'd like to meet.

We sit at a mahogany table outside her home in a garden lined with deep purple Nile lilies and with enormous jacaranda trees overhead, their clusters of large, tubular, lavender-blue flowers covering the entire tree, creating a breathtaking violet spectacle.

I'm unsure where to begin, and say that I think I'm fine, but I've struggled with generalized anxiety, depression, OCD, and mood swings many times in my life, and have been on many medica-tions. I tell her that, though I am coming out of burnout and my muscles tremble regularly, I think I'm stable but would just like to know someone's around in case I go off my rocker, as usual.

She treats me as an equal adult in her demeanor and is respectful and understanding. "It's so wise to speak up before anything goes wrong, because that provides you with an addi-tional cushion of safety. It's not always easy to talk when times are tough, and it's important for people to know you in your strength." She's not letting me off the hook, though. She says,

"Anxiety and depression don't come from nowhere. You make it sound like they just come upon you out of the blue—almost like they're your fault or you're inviting it somehow. Do you mind telling me a little about your childhood?"

I tell her of my idyllic world in New England, the hours playing outside, the weekly rhythms of church and school. I tell her of my love for reading and dreaming. I mention that my parents followed some strict Baptist and Reformed teachings and relate one of my whimsical stories about all four kids being lined up in the bedroom for our ritual communal spankings. I laugh at the memory of us standing oldest to youngest, with my baby sister, who got the lightest touch, wearing three pairs of underwear to cushion the blow. It's nothing I would bat an eye at or find unusual, and I'm not the slightest bit traumatized by the endearing tale.

Florine doesn't laugh. She says, "Christi, it's very important to use correct language about what happened to you. I know your parents might have framed it as Christian spanking, but what you experienced is serious abuse."

The word "abuse" hangs in the air. It's wrong. That's not what happened. My parents loved me, and there wasn't any abuse. I remind her, "My parents are good people. They're thoughtful and generous—my mom even brought me a pre-loaded phone to the airport. They gave me a good education, and there was always food on the table."

She tells me that even good people can badly mistreat their children if they have emotional immaturities and they haven't had the resources they need to learn how to parent gently. When I'm ready, she would like me to be able to say the words: "It was abuse."

I remain unconvinced. I've come to Kenya with the specific intention of forgiving my mom. Calling her a child abuser is no way to begin. I know I was a very difficult, strong-willed child to raise. I was such a rebellious teenager. If I'm to have the joy and freedom I crave, forgiveness is the key.

Over the following years, my mom regularly invites us to leave our kids with them for the weekend so she and my dad can get a chance to spoil them. My parents often tell us they are thrilled to have family nearby at last. She builds a swing set and a sandpit near the house. They live just across the street from a hotel with a beautiful outdoor pool and restaurant. She seems sincere and honestly excited to spend time with them. Maybe she's softened? I hesitate and can't quite bring myself to take her up on the offer for the first couple of years in Kenya, especially while pregnant and nursing Raven, our youngest.

When they invite the kids once again for our wedding anniversary weekend, and Raven's been weaned, we agree. Ben and I haven't been on a weekend adventure alone in ages, and we're excited as we find bags to pack for a camping trip. We borrow a friend's small tent and two sleeping bags, get the kids' things ready, and head to my parents' house.

After dropping off the kids, we say our goodbyes and drive in our rickety Toyota Corolla, with its jacked-up suspension, to Amboseli National Park, a wildlife area known for its vast elephant herds and spectacular views of Mount Kilimanjaro. We're excited to spend time up close and personal with elephants, lions, leopards, and hundreds of species of birds. We're not too interested in giraffes, wildebeest, and zebras, which we can see any day from my parents' backyard.

Arriving at the park campground, we're greeted by a couple of friendly Maasai guards, who tell us we can set up our tent anywhere we like as there are few tourists, especially in small tents. Most people opt for camping cabins or more upscale hotel rooms at the lodges. But I'm a true daughter of my frugal mom, so it's a pup tent for us.

We find the ideal spot, a sandy clearing with no thorns, almost like it's already been swept clean. It's tucked underneath a broad acacia tree. We figure out the tent poles and pegs. I'm satisfied with our handiwork, but Ben insists on turning the overhead flap properly so there's a clear window up to the stars.

We snuggle in the dark, dropping off to chirping crickets, the distant calls of hyenas, and the familiar barking of zebras. Hours later, I'm still asleep, but annoyed that something is pushing hard against my left arm. It feels like a tree has grown right up against the vinyl tent. I push with both hands in my mostly asleep state. "Shoo!"

Ben wakes and whispers, "What are you saying 'shoo' to? That might not be smart." He sits up tall, almost standing, and peers out of the top window to see what's down there. I can hear his breathing stop, as he sinks down next to me. Finger on his lips, he points silently upward. I also half stand to be able to look down from the window. But instead of looking down, I see an enormous eyeball, about a foot away from mine. The shiny, dark iris is only a couple of inches wide, but the eye is set within layers of deeply wrinkled gray skin, creased with dust, so altogether it looks as big as my head. Long eyelashes seem to nearly touch the tent.

I might faint as things fade to gray. My stomach drops to my feet as I think, "If this elephant sits down, we're done for."

We barely move and don't speak. The elephant makes enormous amounts of noise as it tears whole bushes up with its trunk and stuffs the leafy branches into its mouth. The rustling and tearing continue, accompanied by the grinding of vegetation, and a range of snortings and grunts. Motioning to one another, we briefly contemplate making a run for our car, where the risk of being squashed is somewhat lower.

But as we cautiously unzip the tent door, our hungry new companion blocks the entrance. All we can see as we look forward is a long, curved, massive ivory-colored tusk reaching well beyond each side of our tent. We must wait it out. After what seems like hours, our elephant rambles off, and we hear it snuffling as it settles down into a hollow for some loud snoring.

We manage to fall asleep before we're awakened by wild cries of monkeys overhead, and a volley of poop and leaves scattering onto our tent roof. We hear breathing and leaping outside, but don't dare look.

At sunrise, our Maasai guards arrive with coffee and boiled eggs. We excitedly tell them about our nighttime adventures, and they look a little bored. "Yes, we forgot to tell you about Bruno. This is his bed where you've placed your tent. He knows how to open the gate to the camp, but he hasn't slept here in weeks." We ask about the screaming monkeys, and they look at one another, "The only thing that can scare monkeys like that is either a leopard or a python. Those are the two animals that climb trees."

Thankful that our lives have been spared, we spend our day looking at hundreds of elephants from a safer distance. Ten lions rise from the savannah next to our car. Kilimanjaro's snowy peak is as clear as day across the fields of acacias. Altogether, a highly satisfying experience.

We drive back to my parents' place to get the kids, only to find the younger two looking glum, and Micah nowhere to be seen. "What's going on?" I ask my mom. She tells me they had a fun time, but she had to put Micah in time-out. I find that Micah's been locked in a bedroom, so I ask for the key.

When I come into the bedroom, they rush into my arms and burst into tears. I see the same defiant look in their eyes I remember from my childhood. "What happened?" I ask.

Micah shows me an image they've drawn. It's of a small child in a jail, with a large green monster outside the door. They explain, "Grandma asked me if I wanted a banana on my oatmeal, and I said, 'No, I don't like that.' But she said she was giving me a banana in my oatmeal anyway. I couldn't eat it, so she said I had to sit there until I could eat it. But I still couldn't, so she said she'd have to put me in the bedroom until I can obey. But I can't eat it, so I've been in here since breakfast. I tried to come out, but the door is locked. I'm hungry. I tried screaming and banging on the door, but she wouldn't let me out. Then I drew this picture and put it under the door, and she *laughed* at me!"

Despite being locked in a bedroom for more than eight hours, it seems that the laughing is the worst part. I hold my small child close. "I'm so sorry. I'm so sorry, darling. You don't deserve to be treated like that. I promise you that I will never, ever leave you alone for the weekend with her again. It's not funny. Let's get you some food and go home."

We thank my parents for watching the kids, and head for our house. All three kids complain loudly the whole way home, telling us how terrible it was to have Micah locked up, and that nothing they said all day could change Grandma's mind. Leila tells us that she protested that it's not fair—Micah had said no bananas in the first place, and the oatmeal was awful and dry!

It's the first and last weekend the kids will spend in the care of their grandparents. Ben and I decide that we'll continue to go see my parents but not leave the kids with them. We'll be in the house whenever my mom is around. We'll continue inviting them to our house for Thanksgiving, Christmas, and Easter.

For Christmas of 2011, after we've been in Kenya for six years, my parents plan to stay with us for a week. We offer them the cottage we've built as our coaching office in the back garden.

Arriving on Christmas morning, they tell us, "Why don't you stay out in the cottage and sleep in tomorrow, and let us spoil the kids? It will be our gift to you."

I think, "What can go wrong? We're here, close by. We're only sleeping a few steps away."

We exchange gifts on Christmas morning, offering my parents practical things like towels and bathrobes, and giving the kids a stocking full of candy each. We don't do a lot of sweets in our house, so the kids are excited. Our Kenyan friends normally give their kids a new outfit or a pair of shoes for Christmas, and not a lot more, so we keep our gifts in line with what's expected in our neighborhood, and focus on making cinnamon rolls and other foods the kids love.

That evening, Ben and I tuck the kids into bed and head out to our lovely little cottage loft. The following morning, we're awakened by screaming from the house—all three kids are terrified. I listen attentively as I get dressed, buttoning my jeans as I unlock the cottage door. Does my mom have this situation handled?

Fumbling with the lock to the living room, my hands shaking, I rush toward the sounds. My mom is lying under the dining room table, her hands locked around 5-year-old Raven's tiny ankles. Raven is kicking, and clawing at the table legs, shrieking.

I order, "Mom, stand up! What's going on?"

She climbs up, puts her hands on her hips, and says firmly, "Christi, I've just had a run-in with your child." She glares at me, her face bright red, her heart pounding, her breathing irregular.

I say, "What happened?" and she replies, "That kid is so defiant. You have not taught your children to obey their elders, and I'm not going to stand for it anymore."

I ask again what happened, and she tells me that Raven was opening a bag of M&Ms, and she told them not to eat the candy until after breakfast, and they kept opening the bag. So, she grabbed them hard by both arms and set them down hard on the chair, and they bumped their head, but they were fine. She then ordered them to tell her what they wanted to eat, but they refused to answer.

I say, "Mom, that's not okay. You are never to speak to or touch any of my children when you're in a rage."

She takes a huge inhale, and shouts that I always take the kids' side against her, and she can't stand for this anymore. She should have guessed I'd do my permissive parenting thing and let the kids get away with murder.

She walks to the door and calls out to my dad to get his things. To me, she says, "I'm going for a walk to calm down, but I will not stay another minute in this house. We're going."

Slamming the door, she stomps from the house.

After she leaves, Leila speaks up over the other two crying and gasping for breath. "She didn't tell you the whole story, Mom! She picked Raven up by both arms and shook them. Raven was so scared, and I told her to stop. Then she slammed Raven into the chair, and Raven started to scream. She put her whole hand over Raven's mouth and nose and slammed Raven's head into the back of the chair until Raven stopped screaming. Then I started crying because I was scared, and she started yelling at me, too." She continues, "I can't understand how such a little thing could end up with Raven on the floor. It's just M&Ms! Raven was trying to get away from Grandma and fell, and she kept grabbing at Raven's legs while Raven was on the floor. And she was too angry. Usually, I'm happy when Raven gets a spank, but this time I felt pity."

My heart is breaking. For my kids most of all, of course. And for myself. Seeing the violence clearly as an adult is a different experience than wondering if my childhood memories even happened. I've been told my whole life I was the bad one, that I was so difficult and defiant.

The truth is now before my eyes. I know my kids are funny, gentle, kind, silly—they're just regular kids. I know what my mom just did was terribly, terribly wrong.

This is abuse. The word feels true for the first time.

I let the kids know that even firmer boundaries will be in place, and that I'm so, so sorry that I ever left them alone with my mom even for a minute. We will make sure that parents are in the room every second that the grandparents are here.

I walk to my bedroom, where my dad has been relaxing, reading an Agatha Christie novel on my bed. I sit beside him. "Dad, where were you when the screaming was happening?"

"I was reading my book. I figured Grandma had it handled."

"Dad, Mom was the one *causing* the screaming. She had nothing handled! Why didn't you step in?"

He says nothing, just puts his things into his carrying case with a sigh. He meets my mom in front of the house, and they drive away—several days earlier than planned.

The five of us sit in the house, stunned. Ben is furious with my mom. He says little, because he prefers to take a thoughtful, deliberate approach, and doesn't like to rock the boat. He vows in due time to let my parents know exactly how wrong this is. These are his kids, and it's his job to protect them.

For now, we make sure the kids know that nothing that happened is their fault. Adults are not meant to hurt children. We're angry, too.

Raven speaks up, "Mom, I wasn't going to eat the M&Ms, I was just trying to hide them for later!"

Oh, my sweet child. No matter what you were going to do with the M&Ms, the big people need to love and care for the little people.

The next day, I email my parents, *"Mom and Dad. Dear ones. This is not okay. Whether it is simply setting Raven firmly on a padded chair, as you said, while shaking with bottled-up volcanic anger. Or whether it's something more, as the kids said. Either way, Mom, it's not okay. Dad, you must see the truth and be willing to step in. You do not need to agree with our parenting. But we would love to see a real heart change within you both toward active love."*

My mom responds, thanking me for hosting them over Christmas and the thought I put into it. She was sorry the incident with Raven overshadowed an otherwise lovely celebration. She explained she was more confrontational in her approach to child-care and had tried the sweet approach first, but Raven's shouted response to be left alone had pushed her button. Her opinion on what amounts to violence is different to mine, and Raven had not been hurt. She thought what happened showed how much bottled-up frustration and bitterness there was in both of us, which partly came down to how much freedom a child should be given and what kind of restraint should be imposed when they crossed the line. My reaction to my parents shows the harbored bitterness around my childhood, and her volcanic anger that day was from bottling her frustration for too long. She acknowledged at the end of the email that she was too hard on my siblings and me, but that was due to the parenting books supplied by the church when she was a young mother. It should be a balance of tough and soft love, just as God uses both.

The following day, there is a P.S. that none of it was my dad's fault, as he slept through the whole thing and only found out when she had told him about it.

The following year, our mission agency, which loves mavericks and hates rules, decides it needs to put in place a singular policy as it grows to a multi-thousand-person organization. Their sole policy is for Child Protection.

All members are required to watch videos on what can happen to children who encounter abusive adults, before signing the policy. The videos are animations, showing simulated situations in which adults hurt children. I can barely stand to watch. I already know what adults can do to kids, and every muscle in my body is tense as I relive moment after moment of suffering. My hips ache. My jaw aches. My throat aches. My back aches. My esophagus is filled with acid. After completing the requirement, I need to sleep the rest of the day.

Ben and I sit at a table with our area leader, pens in hand, to sign the agency's policy. It states that all members are mandatory reporters, that it has a zero-tolerance policy toward those who abuse children, that it will report to the appropriate civil authorities in the employee's home state, and that it will terminate any employee whose behavior toward a child meets the definition of abuse.

The document lists abusive behaviors in three categories: physical, emotional, and sexual. I can see from reading the list that my mom has done to me one hundred percent of each of the behaviors on the lists of physical and emotional abuse.

When I pick up my pen to sign, I'm promising I will never again leave her with my children for even a moment. I'm promising that henceforth I will call the cops on my mom.

CHAPTER 2

TURNING TOWARD AUTHENTICITY

"You must learn one thing. The world was made to be free in."
David Whyte

As my mom turns from me, I roll my eyes. She can decide if she wants to have seen my pre-teen disrespect or to let it go.

Today, she sees it. Her fingers dig into my arm, and she yanks my shoulder. I feel it pop, as it loosens in its socket.

"Don't you roll your eyes at me, young lady. I could kill you."

I grab onto the yellow vinyl barstool in the kitchen to steady myself, and glance around to see if she's going for the jug of utensils by the stove that holds the wooden spoons. No. She's going to drag me to the bedroom.

With one hand, she twists the skin on my inner arm, hard. I wince and bite my bottom lip. With the other, she twists my arm behind me and pulls me bodily down the hallway toward her room.

Her bedroom is where the more major spankings happen. In her room, she's got a double waterbed covered with my grandmother's beautiful, handmade quilt. Once, my grandmother got to show photos of her quilting to George Bush, when he was governor of Texas. He called her a "national treasure," and none of us has heard the end of it.

Wooden carved lamps top the heavy tables on each side of the bed. Everything is pristine—an oasis of cleanliness in our lived-in house. Near the door to the room is a dresser, where we're entering. Atop the dresser stands a golden upholstered jewelry box, which I see doubled in the mirror. In front of the box, holding pride of place, is "The Stick."

The Stick is set apart, laid perfectly straight on its embroidered cloth across the front of the dresser. Not hidden, never far from sight. We all know what happens if we try to hide it. It travels with us, even on vacation. Its central place gives it weight, even though it's designed to be light and willowy, to give a more sharply noticeable pain—just as *Dare to Discipline* author Dr. James Dobson insisted.

The Stick is not spoken about with tenderness or humor, but with authority, as if this length of wood carries the will of the parent. To look at it inspires fear, even if we kids are just coming into this room to roughhouse on the bed, or to share in a story or a tickling moment.

"I'm going to get The Stick," is the sentence that reminds us instantly of the rule of law and punishment, of the inconsistent, ever-moving line that could not be crossed. Of "she who must be obeyed." And today, its full force is to be felt.

She wields it on every part of my back body, sparing none of her immense strength. I know I should be able to feel it, but I'm not in my body. I think, "This doesn't even hurt."

Maybe I say it out loud, because she screams, "I'll make you feel it this time! I'm going to beat you until you're black and blue.

You won't be able to sit down for a week when I'm done with you! You'll be lucky to be alive."

I don't know how long it will take for her to be done with me. I just know it's going to keep going until I cry and repent. And I am not about to cry and repent. I'm not even here.

My heart is a cold, steely gray. My mind is distant but sharp. When her fury subsides, I stand straight and walk from the bedroom back to the kitchen.

I'm aiming for the phone. It hangs heavy on the kitchen wall, a solid block of plastic in harvest gold, the color of the seventies. The handset rests in its cradle with a long, coiled cord dangling and twisting on itself, stretching just far enough to pace a few steps while talking. The rotary dial will click and whir with each turn, and every number feels deliberate.

I'm finally doing it. I'm calling 911 and telling the police what's happening in our house.

My mom's tread arrives on the linoleum of the kitchen floor. She's cool. Calculating.

"You think you're calling the cops, don't you?" Her face molds into a sneer. "Go ahead. Do it."

She tells me she always knew I'd destroy the household. That if I call the police, they'll have to come and they won't just take me away; they'll take my brother and sisters, too. We'll all be orphans, and they'll never let any of us back home. So, I should do it, if that's what I want.

She leaves the kitchen, and I'm left alone with my finger stuck in the rotary at the number nine. My other arm hangs useless at my side. The flaccid coils of the phone cord droop to the ground.

My legs don't move, though I can feel myself sinking through the floor. My eyes close in defeat, my body empty and power- less. I hang up the phone.

For our wedding, we have a little problem. The problem is mostly me. I really don't like our pastor, who annoys the h*ck out of me with his condescending sermons on Sunday, and his resistance to allowing women to be elected as deacons, which some women in the congregation are pushing for. Currently, the pastors are men, as are the elders, and the deacons, too.

In our church, a deacon's primary role is to lead the church's "ministry of mercy," addressing the material and physical needs of the congregation and community by showing compassion, promoting faithful stewardship, confronting injustice, and organizing acts of service. They serve as model servants who assist the elders by managing the practical concerns of the church, allowing pastors and elders to focus on spiritual leadership and the word of God.

Practically, that means the women visit the sick, make meals for people going through hard times, put out refreshments after the service, and generally take care of everyone. However, they're not allowed to have the deacon title. The elected officials are men, but their wives do much of the work and try to use their influence with their husbands to use the "benevolent fund" in the best ways. They're only asking to be recognized for what they already do and given the resources to carry it out.

No one—not even the most dramatically outspoken of the women—has suggested that women might also know the word of God or be able to teach men. Alongside elders and pastors, deacons serve on the church council. If allowed, they'd be sitting at the same table as men, voting on matters of poverty and global justice. Dangerous, heady stuff!

Our pastor cannot see why women need such budgetary and philosophical power, nor why they care about titles. Sounds like the sin of pride. Next thing you know, they'll be asking to climb the steps to the stage in the front of the sanctuary without the permission of a man. They're already allowed to make announcements about social events. What more could women want?

I can't imagine having this man preach to me about marriage during my double wedding ceremony with my sister when I don't like to listen to him at the best of times. Ben agrees with me, but feels that my inability to just get along with people makes things a lot harder for him. He thinks change takes time, and it's best to move slowly and know the right words to use.

To solve the problem, Ben decides Uncle Abe is the person he'd most like to honor by asking him to offer a homily at our wedding. He's an important figure in Ben's life, having been a "dorm parent" at Ben's boarding school as a missionary kid. He's a kindly, older man who holds a warm place in Ben's heart and who trained Ben in leadership responsibilities as part of dorm life.

Uncle Abe tells us that he never performs a wedding without also providing the pre-marriage counseling. He invites us to his homestead with fruit bushes and a huge sitting lawn mower for a weekend of counsel.

Uncle Abe welcomes us warmly into their home, and Aunt Beatrice offers us piles of refreshments. It feels homey and safe. Until we start talking through the ceremony.

Uncle Abe pointedly asks if I'll say "obey" in my wedding vows.

Well, no! Of course, I'm not going to obey someone for the rest of my life, I think. What an odd, awful thing to sign up for. Maybe our parents bought it, but not us. The day we got engaged, I had majorly panicked. I had seen the way Ben's dad treated his mom, shouting at her to bring him a cup of coffee after his meal, along with a resounding smack on the bottom when she hadn't even sat to eat her meal yet. I sat out on a porch swing with Ben's younger sister, Brenda, wondering, "What have I done? Did I just sign up for a lifetime of servitude in the kitchen?" Brenda assured me that Ben had been trained in washing dishes, doing laundry, and treating women well.

Since the engagement, I had already dreamily started planning the personal vows that I'd like to write—promises of saying yes to one another as often as possible, having as much fun and joy as we can muster in good times and bad, and keeping the romance alive.

Today, I glance over at Ben, feeling a little desperate. He's a lot better at being diplomatic. I'd probably blast the h*ck out of Uncle Abe, who I'm meeting for the first time, and we'd never get married. As usual, Ben has come prepared. He knows exactly what to expect. He knows me and he knows Uncle Abe.

Ben opens the hymnbook he's brought from our church and finds the wedding vows in the back pages. "We'd really prefer to use the vows that are already sanctioned by our home church. You can see that there's mutual submission in these vows."

I grind my teeth, smiling tightly. I had really wanted to express my own words, not read out of a book. But if I don't have to vow to obey anybody, that's a move in the right direction.

Uncle Abe decides that, with us, he's got a problem case on his hands. He strategizes that he'll take Ben out to the fields for some manly grunt-work and a talk about headship, while he leaves me in the capable hands of Aunt Beatrice in the kitchen. Before the men leave, he tells a hilarious story about how his wife hadn't been too sure about obedience at first, either. The first time he gave her a command that she resisted, he tells us, "I picked her up and set her on top of the refrigerator! I didn't let her come down until she promised to do what I had asked." They both laugh uproariously, while I feel my insides shrinking into a tight ball. Uncle Abe rounds this off, "Think how much more relaxing it will be when you don't have to make so many decisions. All those worries can be transferred to your husband, who cares for you so much."

After the men leave, Aunt Beatrice is all warm smiles, pouring me tea, and laying out lovely napkins. She has a story of her own, "Imagine you're a 4-year-old girl. You're having a wonderful time playing with your ball in the front yard, and it goes rolling out into the street. You run to catch it, but your mother is watching. She's stronger and wiser than you. She sees you're about to be seriously hurt, so she rushes forward and snatches you from danger, just before a car comes down the street! That child needs to learn to obey immediately, and to trust in the parent's wisdom. You can see that having an older, wiser person can keep you from so many problems!"

She has rested her case. I fail to see the analogy between a small child being protected by an adult, and a grown woman being in a lifelong partnership with a man. I have no words. At all.

I'm doing my best not to upset the apple cart. Smoothing things over seems to be the only way to go, so I make some ambiguous sounds, hoping my head won't explode, and desperately wishing Ben would return. I know for sure that anything I might say would have no impact, but if I can convince Ben to advocate for me, we have a chance.

When we have a moment alone, I whisper fiercely to Ben, "We'd better not have any talk about obedience at the ceremony! That would upset so many people. Can you imagine if Uncle Abe preaches about Ephesians 5, given everything going on at church these days? You've got to tell him clearly!"

I don't dare push my luck with my desires to write my vows, but I'm certainly not going to throw the women of my church under the bus—this feels bigger than me. We have a history with good old Ephesians 5, a chapter in the Bible used throughout history to subjugate women. "Wives, submit to your husbands as to the Lord" (verse 22) has historically been lifted and used out of context to argue that women should obey their husbands unquestioningly.

In our church and the Baptist church my parents attended previously, this verse is framed as a hierarchical order, with men being the "head" (verse 23) in a way that gives them authority and leadership over women. This is the exact passage my church cited to justify restricting women's roles in the church, not just keeping them from leadership or ordination as pastors, but also from the lowly deacon role. These few verses have also been misused to silence women in cases of abuse, with the idea that enduring mistreatment was part of faithful submission.

I couldn't tell you why any of that was wrong, just that my own rebellious heart knew it to be wrong in a fiery, passionate, helpless way. Ben helped me out by researching the egalitarian position—instead of starting the reading at verses 22 and 23, he goes back to the previous verse, which calls all believers to "submit to one another out of reverence for Christ." This frames the entire section as mutual, not one-directional.

Ben has always preferred to use his power as a white, Christian American man and his prodigious life-long study of scripture to beat people at their own game and bring more equality to the world. When we got engaged and Ben had returned from Liberia to our house, my older brother took him out for a morning of canoeing on the pond, determined to have a man-to-man conversation about headship and submission.

"Before I can give you permission to get engaged," my brother said, despite us already being engaged and no one feeling the need to consult him, "I need you to exegete Ephesians 5 for me. I need to know that you can be the true head of your home and that you can get Christi to submit to you. She's so headstrong, and you seem to be too much of a pushover."

Ben answered firmly and quietly, "It's my job to love my wife as Christ loves the church, and to be willing to lay down my life for her. Christi's an adult. It's her job to read her own Bible and interpret the verses about submission for herself."

Ben had versed himself in a radical, emerging way of thinking called "egalitarianism." In this view, Saint Paul redefines "headship" not as domination but as sacrificial love. That kind of "headship" is about service, not control. This new reading of Ephesians 5 was radical in its time, giving dignity and worth to wives in a culture where women had little power. Egalitarians argue that the ultimate vision is mutuality—love, respect, and mutual submission—reflecting Christ's way of being in a relationship. Egalitarians connect this text to broader biblical themes, like in Galatians 3:28: "There is neither male nor female, for you are all one in Christ Jesus," to show that hierarchy isn't the gospel's goal.

I had never even heard of egalitarianism and had no stomach for the mental gymnastics of trying to make all the different Bible verses fit into coherent themes. I just couldn't stand always having to do what men thought was right, even if they were stupid. But I was fist-pumping thrilled that my soon-to-be-husband had a bachelor's degree in biblical studies and a lifetime as a missionary to finally be able to stand up to my brother with some power.

I knew Ben would have a way to talk with Uncle Abe from his own arsenal and convince him to leave this obedience thing alone on our wedding day. As promised, before we left at the end of the weekend, Ben speaks with him directly and firmly, saying that our one request was that he preach from the Psalms rather than from Ephesians. I am relieved and impressed that my man could go head-to-head biblically against such nonsense.

The day of our wedding arrives. My sister, Kathryn, and I are equally excited. Neither of us wanted to be the center of attention on our wedding day, and a double wedding allows us to have fun together. She also had no interest in having our pastor give her homily, so she's invited another young pastor named John, who has the radical idea that love is meant to be at the heart of a marriage partnership.

The ceremony begins with a comedy of errors. My mom has just as hard a time with this headship thing as I do. She insists she should be the one to walk me down the aisle, not my dad, because she raised me, while he lazed around reading the newspaper. And furthermore, no man was going to give away her daughter to another man, when she had done all the work.

There is no way I am letting my mom walk me down the aisle. I want my dad by my side on our big day as I always feel safe and happy with him. But to mollify my mother, and my own sense of justice, we decide that instead of the pastor saying, "Who gives this woman to this man…" and my dad responding, "Her mother and I do," we will have both parents stand and offer their blessing on the marriage.

This is a new page in Uncle Abe's playbook. He must change the script not just once, but for both brides. Confusing! There is some point where we were all supposed to say, "With God's help, we will." He has "Kathy" (my sister only goes by Kathryn) marrying Ben, and me marrying her fiancé. He has the wrong parents blessing the wrong kids' marriages. Finally, he cracks and says, "With God's help, *we will* make it through this wedding!" The congregation roars.

The time comes for the homily. Uncle Abe begins, "Ben asked me not to preach on Ephesians 5 or on submission, but I prayed about it and just knew that this is exactly the passage that this couple needs most. The Psalms might have been more palatable, but this couple needs the truth!" Then he dives right in with an impassioned speech, "The more love (on the part of the husband), the more submission (on the part of the wife). The more submission, the more love!" He extolls the virtues of proper hierarchy and headship and says, "Christi, at the end of this sermon, if I've convinced you that obeying and submitting to your husband is God's truth for you, you will say, I do."

I panic. Will I really have to fight with this guy in front of the whole church at my wedding? Or will I build my marriage vow on a lie that I agreed with this miserable excuse for a human? My heart races. Blood floods my cheeks. I stand, frozen, with a pasted-on smile. I can feel the tension rise across the congregation. The women here have heard this rhetoric too many times. They are silently angry with him along with me. I can feel it.

At the end of the homily Uncle Abe reads a simple sentence out of the scripture, "If you take this man to be your husband say I do." I choke out "I do" without also appearing to agree with every word of his interpretation of the scripture.

And then Ben is allowed to kiss me. And it is a lovely kiss. He takes my face in both hands, tenderly, looks deeply into my eyes, and lingers over the kiss. This is a man promising to cherish me, hold me, and honor me as his equal. The congregation let out an audible, "Awwwwww," and we all relax.

I'm in the chapel at the university I volunteer at in Kenya—Africa International University outside of Nairobi. It's the largest room on campus, which can hold hundreds of people and there's a palpable buzz. As a volunteer in the communications department, I'm invited to join the university faculty and staff to meet a professional coach for the first time.

The tall, vibrant, jet-black-haired Canadian coach Suzanne stands in all her feminine power and authority in front of a group of men and women. She and her husband are incredibly good-looking, and he's beaming in support of his wife.

Overhead, a concrete, beam-reinforced roof slopes from above the center stage to a lower point around the curved entrances to the back. About two hundred of us stand with our completed DISC scores in sealed envelopes, ready to be guided through an interactive workshop.

The four DISC categories—Dominance, Influence, Steadiness, and Conscientiousness—describe behavioral styles and tendencies of equal value and usefulness. The idea is that we'll open our envelopes and sort ourselves into the four categories, each having been given a large space in the room where the vibe of each type will become amplified and obvious.

Those high in Dominance are results-focused and assertive, while those high in Influence are enthusiastic and persuasive. People with high Steadiness are patient, cooperative, and dependable, and those with high Conscientiousness focus on accuracy, expertise, and quality.

I open my envelope with nervous excitement, thinking I might be an Influencer, and pretty sure Steadiness is not going to be in my top quadrant. I discover I'm a D for Dominant and am curious to join my squad of inspiring high achievers in the quadrant with a giant Lion poster.

I can see the other quadrants are forming. The "Is" for Influence include about fifty people, and their part of the room emanates enthusiasm, optimism, warmth, and relational energy. They're talking and laughing, slapping one another on the back, offering high fives, and genuinely enjoying one another's company. Their vibrancy is palpable, and they're clearly pleased with the poster of the friendly otters holding hands overhead. I would love to join them.

The "S" space feels different. These steady folks exude a sense of cooperation, sincerity, and dependability. They look as patient and harmonious as the cooing dove on the poster over their heads. They've found their space quietly and organize themselves thoughtfully. They keep their voices down and look like the types you'd want to collaborate with before making any sudden moves. You'd want to be gentle with these folks.

The "C" crowd, for Conscientiousness, has its own deliberative calm. If I had a spreadsheet that needed an accuracy check, I'd head right over there. These guys look like they'd need a lot of data to be influenced about anything. You can almost feel the skepticism even among themselves, almost like they want to look at one another's scorecards to ensure things have been done correctly, and that you're really meant to be in this square. My judgy-self dismisses them quickly as they're going nowhere fast. Yikes—I know that's not where I belong.

But where are my people, the "Ds"? We're supposed to be the ones who take charge and make things happen. We're nice and social, right? But there's no one over here in the D space—except a tall Maasai guy generally known on campus to be a jackass. He says, "Hi, Christi!" and attempts to shake my hand. But I'm stunned. I'm already the only white person in the room, besides the Canadian coach, and I'm already one of the few women. And why are there only two of us in this section of the room, when the other three squares have about fifty people each?

Who wants a dominant woman? No one I've ever met. I stand there trying to orient myself. I can sense the curiosity as people in the other parts of the room eye us two mean jerks. I can hardly move. Before tears burst from my eyes, I run from the room out the back doors and stand doubled over in the grassy center of campus, trying to get an intake of breath.

I suddenly recognize myself in those childhood stories. I am evil, unlovable, worthy of fire and brimstone. I'm not even a real woman. And probably not a Christian. I'm a misfit and an outcast. I wreck everything. I can't go back inside that chapel.

I look up and I see the coach, Suzanne, standing brightly in front of me. She's kind. She's strong. She's got the data to prove that Ds are part of things, too. She puts her hands warmly on each of my shoulders. She looks in my eyes and says, "Christi, I see your tender heart."

I can feel my tender heart bursting as she speaks.

CHAPTER 3

THE TRAIL OF SELF-COMPASSION

"I am asking you to hold the parts of you that shatter, that scare you, close."

Nikita Gill

My mom is bending over her bed, which is neatly made, as always, with my grandmother's quilt. Her bottom is high in the air, and her head buried in the pillows. I am around 9 years old and it is a disturbing view.

Mom stretches out her right arm to me, holding The Stick.

"Spank me! I deserve it. I must have been a terrible mom to have had such an awful child as you. Why do you kids hate each other so much? I must be a bad mom. I'm the one who deserves it. Please! Spank me!"

Tempted for a brief, rageful moment to slam her with the stick, I melt into compassion, sobbing, and hugging her.

"No, you're a *great* mom! I'm the bad one."

For a time, my two sisters and I share one bedroom between us so we can use the other room as a playroom and go wild with our imaginings. We build a fantastical boat of cushions, blankets, and the usual fort-building paraphernalia.

As usual in our incredibly real, made-up world, the storm is fierce, and our comfy boat is engulfed by huge waves. The howling wind means we need to shout to be heard. I stand strong, pulling on ropes and masts with all my might to ensure my little sisters are safe.

We each take on a persona of a boy called Johnny. I am "13-year-old Johnny," the biggest, toughest, bravest of them all. My sisters choose other Johnnys that day, such as "6-year-old Johnny" and "10-year-old Johnny" who are all older and stronger than we three little girls.

Together, with me at the helm, we might be safe from the gigantic threats bearing down upon us from every direction. If I let my guard down for even a moment, we will all be drowned. It is my job to keep them safely in the boat. With urgency, I direct the movements to keep them from sliding too close to the edge.

My youngest sister, however, has no regard for our safety. Filled with fearful compassion, she sees one of her hundreds of plastic dolls lying on the floor and cries, "Oh, no! There's a baby in the waves; we must save her!" Leaning too far off the edge, she risks life and limb.

Engulfed by terror, I shout, "Leave the baby! It's just a stupid doll. We must save ourselves first. If anyone else joins our boat, all our lives are in danger!"

But again, she gives no heed. Forty, fifty times over she brings another of her plastic figures into the boat that is barely strong enough to hold us. Soon, it is ready to capsize, such is its ballast.

Taking full control of the situation, I see it all clearly. I must save the real, live sisters. I must throw the plastic weight into the tossing water. Making the most difficult decision on my own, I throw the dolls by the armload back into the seas, while my youngest sister weeps bitterly.

My mom entered the room. "Christi!" she shouts angrily. "You are so mean. Can't you see that your sister is crying? How dare you throw those dolls into the water. Can't you see that to her they are real babies? What is wrong with you? How did I raise such a terrible daughter?"

She takes me off to her bedroom for a good, hard spank. "Now, go into your room alone and think about what you've done. Don't come out until you can apologize and play nicely with your sisters."

My butt stinging, and my heart stinging worse, I sit in my room and turn to bitter stone. I am unable to speak. Unable for my reality to be seen or heard. The storm is as dangerous as ever, and I am helpless to do anything about it.

Twenty years later, I'm the mom, learning to re-parent myself. In my imagination, I enter my childhood room filled with drama and see three little girls, each one just as cherished and lovable as the next.

Recognizing the fear, the drama, the shouting, I become the calm in the storm. I see little Christi, so small, but believing herself to be so strong.

I gently join them in the boat. Wordlessly, I let them know I'm here. We're all safe. We're all loved. While the storm rages on, I gently invite my younger self onto my lap. "Sweet little Christi," I whisper, caressing her hair. "You're such a wonderful person. I see you. I love you. You've done enough. We're okay. I've got this. You can relax."

As Christi settles in for a warm cuddle, safe in my arms, my youngest sister begins rescuing babies. It's okay. Plenty of love and safety in the storm for the real, live daughters. There's plenty of room on our boat. The good mom is there.

Jessica and I meet in kindergarten class. A sweet, bubbly, freckled redhead, she is always laughing and moving quickly. She makes me want to twirl and dance.

Her house is on Beech Drive, which I think is a beautiful name. Our playdates are always at her house, where her short, vivacious mom Amanda bustles around, humming. When Jessica's dad comes home, he wears an impish grin and the two parents kiss and talk in the kitchen. Her family is always cooking up plans—heading to Block Island, going to her family's cottage, or to an amusement park. Their conversations turn around fun times at the lake, boating, and puppies.

Jessica's mom loves coming up with activities for the two of us. One day we bake chocolate chip cookies. Jessica's method is to leave out the chocolate chips until the scoops of dough are ready, then she adds exactly four chocolate chips to each cookie, not too close together. According to her, that is the exact chocolate-to-dough ratio that leads to the most delicious outcomes. Another day, it is paper dolls. We punch out dresses with tabs all around to fold over the underwear-clad figures. There are always craft supplies available for our coloring creations. I arrive home feeling happy and refreshed, like all is right in the world.

Jessica teaches me the basics: when you go to the bathroom, always wipe from front to back and when you wipe the back, reach behind you. Every time you pee, wash your hands afterwards. When you make a sandwich, you can put two or even three slices of deli meat on it, as well as cheese. She is an endless source of life lessons from her mom.

My mom warns me about Jessica's family, "Not everyone who goes to your school is actually a Christian, you know. Some people don't take it seriously. They're more like social Christians, and their lives don't reflect it. They spend their money on fun instead of giving to the poor. Remember Jessica's family only goes to church on Sunday mornings. I don't even see them at the evening service, let alone Wednesday night Bible study. And I heard that they don't go to church at all in the summer when they're on holiday. Just be careful you don't get too sucked into their worldly life that you lose sight of what's important."

In sixth grade, Jessica breaks my heart. One day, she comes to me rather sheepishly to say, "I don't want to be best friends anymore." I have no idea how to respond. How could I have not seen this coming? Best friends are always best friends, aren't they?

I manage to stumble out, "Why? What did I do?"

Her response is clear. She explains that Ashley is more fun and cooler. She knows more about boys. Jessica adds that she doesn't understand my jokes.

That is that. I have lost to the most popular girl in our class. The playdates are over, and I am bereft. The rest of sixth grade passes in relative peace, but the sparkle is gone. Instead of stopping by Jessica's house on the way home from school, I go straight home. Two other girls in the class, Stephanie and Heather, are quiet and reserved but kind enough to let me hang out with them in the uncool area, to the side of where the other girls play dodgeball, twirl their hair, and watch the boys on the soccer field.

Our teacher makes school fun. We spend hours drawing castles, complete with a moat, the keep, the tower, and the crenelated battlements, and surrounded by fields, serfs, and horse-mounted knights. She reads heroic historical tales of Europe while we draw. I am considered the most responsible person in class and run errands for her. Being the teacher's pet does little for my social standing.

Growing increasingly frustrated that the girls aren't interesting to talk to, I start playing soccer with the boys. I can outrun most of them and be counted on to pass the ball. One day, the class sets up a one-hundred-yard dash between the fastest boy and the fastest girl—me. We sprint with all our might and end in a tie, both of us insisting we have won.

Seventh grade begins with quiet misery but relative hopefulness. I am the youngest in the class by far. The second youngest, Sasha, is invariably polite and I had been to her house a few times over the summer. Stephanie and Heather still talk with me at recess. I have learned to French-braid hair, a highly sought-after skill in the girls' bathroom at lunchtime, so I fit in a little better than I do on the soccer field.

A new girl has come to town who strikes terror in my heart. Tiffany is entirely sure of herself, speaking with lawyerly authority on all subjects and arriving with power and command. Nearly immediately, she susses out who the leader of the girls is—Ashley, who my former best friend Jessica had dumped me for. They form an alliance. The Ashley-and-Tiffany duo changes the power dynamic, and I suffer to watch Jessica pushed to the sidelines after only one year of favor.

Quiet, sensitive Heather is the first to be ostracized—no one is to invite her to the group activities, lest she contaminate the rest of us with her lack of coolness. This enrages me, and I deliberately spend more time with her, the two of us sitting aside chatting quietly while the others laugh and joke.

Befriending Heather is my downfall. I am the next target. I had thwarted Tiffany's authority, and my low-level mutiny would not go unpunished. I start to notice whispering going on until one day, Ashley and Tiffany get all the girls to line up in the playground for an official ostracizing ceremony. They create an oath that each girl promises never to speak to me again. All who agree line up and walk past me, held between Ashley and Tiffany, and say, "I promise."

Most of the girls look bored as they walk past, each saying "I promise" nonchalantly. Stephanie is distraught. She bursts into tears. "I don't want to promise. I'm so sorry, Christi. But I just have to. I promise."

Last is Jessica. Her face pale, her voice somber, she looks at the ground and quietly says, "I promise."

For the remainder of that year, none of the girls, other than Heather, speak a word to me between classes, at lunch, or after school. I am completely isolated. My emotions swing wildly between devastation and anger. I think to myself repeatedly, "These idiots don't know what they're missing. I'm creative, funny, great at drawing, and more fun than any of them. They are the ones missing out." And another part of me whispers, "You're a nerd. You're bad. You deserve this. You are uniquely and completely defective."

Around that time, I am heading home on the bus one day and I get in an argument with someone who isn't letting me sit by them in their double seat. "You're such an idiot!" I cry out. My mom happens to be standing outside the bus and hears. She comes onto the bus and yanks my arm, dragging me outside. "Don't you ever let me hear you talking like that again! Just because you're smarter than everyone else gives you no right to call them idiots. You need to learn some humility, young lady!"

I acquire debilitating headaches and stomachaches each morning before school. At first, my mom thinks I am faking it and makes me go to school, but over time she can see me losing all energy and my face growing pale. I struggle to eat. She lets me stay home and each evening brings my assignments home from my teachers for the following day.

I build a comforting routine. Wake up with a headache, don't eat breakfast, stay home. As soon as the rest of our family leave for school, my headache dissipates, I finish my schoolwork in less than an hour and have a glorious day free to read and draw by myself. I lounge on the back deck, swing on a rope in the woods, and keep myself entertained with my thoughts and drawings.

The routine is not to last, though, as my mom involves doctors in discovering the source of the headaches. I know exactly what is causing them, but there is no way anyone could drag the shameful story from me.

We spend a lot of time in waiting rooms. One doctor takes a long time asking strange questions that don't seem to have anything to do with my physical health. One of his questions is, "Do you ever see things that other people don't see?" And I immediately answer, "Yes." He perks up. "Like what kinds of things?" he probes. "Well, you know bugs and flowers and moss. I tend to look down a lot and I like to look at plants. I'm the first person to notice when there's a lady slipper blooming in the woods. Everyone else seems to look up at each other's faces, so they miss things." The doctor's body collapses back into apathy.

My mother explains to me afterwards that his question was designed to see if I was hallucinating. It becomes a family joke around the dinner table. "Hey, do you ever see things that other people don't see?" "Yes, *bugs*! Ha, ha, ha, ha, ha, ha, ha!"

During our various doctor visits, my mom decides I am old enough to fill out my own medical forms, so she walks me through which boxes to check, mostly a long list of "no" answers. Until we got to broken bones and she tells me I did break a bone when I was two. My right clavicle.

"Really, how did I manage to break a bone? Did I fall from something?"

"Hmmm, that's a good question. I don't remember it at all. You were getting your diaper changed and it broke."

"Well, what did the doctor say? What kind of treatment did I get?"

"It was a long time ago, and I really don't recall any of that."

I feel dread and mild unease, deciding it is better not to wonder how a 2-year-old breaks her own clavicle.

The umpteenth doctor checks all my vitals and then asks my mom to leave the room. My mom fights this valiantly but the doctor holds firm. "Sometimes kids speak more freely when a parent isn't around. I promise she'll be safe."

Alone, the doctor looks at me with her kind eyes and uses a soft tone. "Honey, I just wonder if there's any bullying going on at school. Could you just nod your head if that's the case? You don't have to say anything you don't want to." My eyes fill with tears, and she keeps gazing at me gently. "Girls can be very mean at that age. If there's something happening, it's not your fault, it just means that you're not in a safe environment." I tell her nobody at school is hitting me, but she insists, "Bullying with girls doesn't always look like that. It can look like the silent treatment also. Could it be something like that?"

I nod slowly. "Please don't tell my mother."

She promises to do what is in my best interest.

When my mom returns, the doctor says, "I think Christi needs a different environment. Would you be willing to look at other schools in the area? She would do better in a different classroom."

My mom is incensed, "We put her in the best private Christian school! We've built our whole lives around that. It's like our family. I work there. All the rest of the kids go there. I am not putting one of my children in a public school. There's no telling what goes on in schools like that."

The doctor persists, "Another class within the same school then. Are there several seventh-grade classes?" Our school is small with less than thirty kids per grade.

"What if you held her back a year? She's the youngest in her class, and it couldn't hurt to let her grow socially for a bit." My mom decides that is ridiculous. "Christi is highly gifted. She wins the reading award every year, and gets straight As. If anything, she could skip a year."

The plot to skip a year begins. My mom speaks to each of my seventh-grade teachers and asks them if I could handle jumping ahead. It takes determination and much debate to decide if it is the best plan, especially as it hasn't been done before. In the end, after a summer of discussions, all are convinced.

I begin eighth grade with my class. After a few days of eighth grade, I am asked to return my textbooks to my teachers. Someone announces I will be joining the class above, and I am asked to follow the high school principal down the hall to my new classroom. I don't recall saying any goodbyes to the eighth grade, just leaving silently.

Beginning ninth grade a few days later, my whole body is shaking. I decide my best defense is to disappear as completely as possible. I sit toward the back and try to figure out who is nice and who is not.

The tall, blond, talkative girls who spend time with curling irons before school, and can flirt effortlessly with the boys, seem the most dangerous. I am 12 and they are 14 and tower over me. The gulf between us seems enormous.

In science class, I am seated at a desk for right-handers. The L-shaped surface was created to cradle the right arm and leave space to the left for the student to sit. I take notes awkwardly with my left, with no space for my elbow. I drop my pencil off the right side. The tallest basketball player, Justin, sits just to my right. His long legs drape over the space between us. I briefly consider asking him to hand me my pencil, but I am too terrified to speak. I lean as far as I can over the armrest and the desk slips from its moorings. I find myself and my books splayed on the floor. The whole class turn to look and erupt into laughter. Justin helps me up.

In French class, we learn adjectives. Each of us in turn says a sentence like, *"Justin est fort."* Week after week, the only adjective anyone can think of to describe me is, *"Christi est timide."* I think, "I'm *not* timid!" But I am scared out of my mind every day.

On the first day of my senior year in high school, my invisibility cloak has become so complete that one of the most popular girls, a kind, bouncy, blond cheerleader, walks over to me confidently, "Hi, I'm Nicole! Welcome to our school! I'm so glad you're here and I'm happy to show you around."

I'm stunned—this is my twelfth year at this school, and our class has only twenty-nine students. I can't even be seen.

Sister Pat, who I first met at the Ignatian spiritual retreat, which resulted in her meeting me every month for the following five years, tells me over again, month after month, that I'm not to blame. I'm not responsible for the actions, emotions, or thoughts of others.

It's hard for this to sink in. Whenever my husband Ben looks at me with a furrowed brow, I panic. My body shrinks, and he appears enormous as I frantically go through all the possibilities of how I might have messed up and brought his anger upon myself. My emotions are dramatically outsized, and my body stays in a state of alert. My hips throb in pain, my glutes seize up, and my stomach clenches.

Ben's not too thrilled with my vigilant stance and gently offers that there's an EMDR training for counselors happening in Nairobi. My counselor friends Kerri and Bethany are both taking the course, and I decide to be a guinea pig for their new skills.

Bethany is gentle. As we begin, she takes a brief history and explains that Eye Movement Desensitization and Reprocessing, EMDR, is a simple, structured process that will not be too traumatizing and will bring relief. It won't change my memories, but the right-left brain integration will remove the physical and emotional effects I've been suffering.

As we start, she offers me a couple of grounding practices in case things get overwhelming. She sits on a chair facing me and explains she'll be moving her two fingers back and forth in front of my eyes as I return to a stressful memory, and that she'll prompt me on what to do. At first, I think I'll have her help me with a more recent mugging, but at the last minute, I change my mind and tell her I want to do my mom's "Spank Me" incident, which is the most contortionist, blood-chilling story of my childhood. She tells me that she's very sorry for my experience and allows her eyes to get bright with tears.

I can barely think or speak about this incident without going into spasms of pain. We identify that my level of distress around the event is near ten, and that my belief that I'm evil and deserve punishment feels very real to me. We identify that a goal for the session will be for me and my body to believe I'm safe now.

As I speak, Bethany's fingers move back and forth. I can remember thoughts, feelings, sensations, and images from the room. Somehow, it's less distressing than before. We pause and think through what this incident might mean. Does it really mean I'm evil? Well, maybe not. It does seem like a little kid can't be that bad.

We repeat the same story, with another round of looking left and right, following her fingers. At our next pause, the story seems quite odd. I don't think I could have done anything bad enough to make this make sense.

We do the third and fourth round. With the fourth telling of the story, I break into peals of laughter! I can still see the same images, remember the same thoughts, but it feels so different. The whole thing is ridiculous! I feel overwhelmed with an enormous overflow of hilarity, love, wisdom, and compassion for both little me and my mom. We were in such a tangle! She had so few resources. I was so small. None of it could have meant anything other than a mom who was exhausted and confused and unloved, and a little girl who wanted and deserved to be loved by someone who couldn't.

There's no distress now. My body feels clear and calm as Bethany and I scan it together. It's like I can see the data, but it's just data. The quilt is still there. The stick is still in my mom's hand. But it's pretty funny.

It doesn't even seem like there's anything to forgive. There's no reason for blame. My mom is responsible for herself, her emotions, and behaviors. What she did was wrong, but it was on her. I was a child, who was meant to be cherished.

Not only am I safe now, but I'm so darn lovable. I see that little girl, so full of love that it spills out even in the worst misery and confusion. I can see she behaved out of a childlike protective mechanism, and I can also see that this kid is amazing. That little girl is much stronger than she knows. I break into a huge grin.

I'm stronger and more loving than I ever knew.

I'm probably the first one to sign up for Brené Brown's 2015 training in London to become a *Certified Daring Way Facilitator*. She has never offered her course outside of the United States before, and only about forty spaces are available. I'm excited to travel to London to spend a week with her and her team, and then the next eighteen months digging into the work. I've read all her books and gone through *The Gifts of Imperfection* class on the Oprah Winfrey Network.

I'm enthralled by her introduction to Kristin Neff's work on self-compassion and go down a rabbit hole to learn all I can. I realize the voice in my head is so often a voice of condemnation, put-downs, judgments, sarcasm, and negativity. It's easy to be positive, warm, compassionate, and complimentary toward others—even to a fault—but to myself I say things like:

"I look like a hippo."

"Who am I to coach people when I'm so morose all the time?"

"I have no idea what I'm doing."

I certainly would never dream of saying them to someone else, but as I watch every video I can find from Kristin Neff, I realize those are the words running through my head on auto-pilot. The good news is I'm causing my own pain, and I can stop it.

It's not easy, but I begin with writing myself page after page of what Kristin calls "Compassionate Whispers." I make simple drawings with the whispers to cement the kind words. I see myself walking around, with bubble quotes over my head, saying, "Honey, you're tired. Everyone goes through highs and lows in their business sometimes. You don't know everything, but you're learning." Or "Sweetie pie, you do get down and sad sometimes. That's human. And you're also one of the most loving, compassionate people I know."

I dream up terms of endearment for myself, the same ones I use for my kids and my closest friends. My calendar each Monday pops up with several hours off. The message, "Time to start the week creatively, slowly and mindfully, my darling!"

I discover more each day that when I speak to myself with kindness and warmth in the second person (instead of judging in the first person) it's way better for my mental health. I can see myself as part of common humanity, worthy of self-kindness, and mindfulness.

Something about taking the position of a friend helps. If I say, "I am burned out," that has a different feel than, "You are burned out, sweetheart." Just that little distance, that little extra perspective, looking at myself with the eyes of a friendly, neutral party.

Instead of asking how I feel *about* myself, I ask how I feel *toward* myself. Can I feel a little bit softer, a little bit more friendly toward this person, who is me, who is doing the best she can? Who's imperfect and infinitely lovable.

CHAPTER 4

THE EROSION OF DISSOCIATION

*"The breeze at dawn has secrets to tell you.
Don't go back to sleep!"*
Rumi

My childhood spot is in the living room, on the red and gold plaid upholstered couch with the hand-knit green and white throw blanket. I sit for hours, my arm draped over the back, facing the bay window out toward the street. The thriving spider plant with multiple babies and the African violet hang over my head in their macrame hangers. A tired philodendron with an inexplicable faded Italian flag stuck in dry soil sits in its pot below.

I have three main activities on this couch, depending on stress levels. One is to sit frozen in a panic making up strange games for my mind. When I see a car is coming down the hill, which only happens a few times each afternoon, if I manage to fly down the stairs (literally fly, because I am really Peter Pan, and I do have this power) and touch my hand to the front door while ducking my head underneath the window before the car gets to our driveway, then no one in my family will die. I always manage to get there in time, my feet thumping loudly on the landing after I fly down the seven steps.

On days when there is less clenching in my stomach, I opt for dreaming about heaven. Heaven is the highest place, the holiest place, a cloudy paradise where there is no weeping or gnashing of teeth. It's conditionally accessible by earthly beings who display goodness, piety, and faith. I've been told by the two pastors' sons in my third-grade class that I will make an excellent pastor's wife someday. Before Jason Timber's father gets transferred to a pastorate in Michigan, he gives me a parting gift, a book called *Ten Great Women of the Bible*, assuring me I'm the most virtuous girl he knows, and would definitely be woman number eleven. So, there's reason to hope.

My most peaceful activity is to get lost in a book. In *The Secret at Pheasant Cottage*, by North African missionary Patricia Saint John, an English girl, Lucy, who has lived with her grandparents since she was little, has dim memories of someone else. She knows her grandparents are hiding something. She's a determined girl, and eventually finds her father, who's recently been released from prison. On her adventures with him in Spain, she learns to "never, never hate." I read this same book at least eighty times. The spine is cracked and torn. Living her adventures, I'm filled with Lucy's apprehensions, joys, and grief each time.

Often, my mom admonishes me, "You're reading too much. It's time for you to get outside. You're going to end up needing glasses." I manage to tuck my book inside my pants before heading out the door. Outside, I have two favorite spots. If the house feels dangerous, I can sit behind a large boulder behind the woodpile at the edge of the woods. No one can see me here, and I can continue reading on a damp pile of leaves.

My favorite place on earth is with my dearest friend, the Eastern hemlock tree, which stands directly to the left of our house, guarding my carefully tended rock garden below. The circumference of its trunk is at least twice the length of my arms, and its purplish-brown bark is deeply grooved and furrowed with flat-topped scaly ridges that leave marks on my arms when I hug it tight. It's more than three times the height of our house and shaped like an enormous pyramid, its upper-crown narrow and willowy, its wide canopy of lower branches covered with tiny, dense cones the size of the tip of my pinky hanging from each branch tip.

I long to climb it. My big brother has built a three-step ladder out of five boards. He uses it to climb to the first branch, and quickly pulls the ladder up after him so I can't follow. He sits mocking me from a few branches up. But, when I'm 8 years old, I triumph. Getting a running start, I take two swift strides up the trunk, my bare feet landing firmly, and I fling my arms and torso upward to take hold of a short, broken bough that's less than a foot long. Hanging there, I manage to scrabble my legs over this smooth, dead branch until I can pull myself to safety onto a firmer branch further up.

Once I'm standing there, the tree is mine. I have no fear, I can use my knees, hands, feet, and chin to scurry past my brother, who clings below me. I continue climbing far beyond where anyone would think safe, to the topmost branches where the trunk is the width of my spindly leg, and sways dizzyingly in the wind. I look down at our rooftop, on all the other oaks and maples, and onto the pond in the distance. My stomach turns if I look straight down, but my heart races when I keep my eyes on the horizon. Grasping the trunk between my thighs and hanging on for dear life, I can tell my sweet hemlock tree all the day's woes.

In 1980, when I'm 9 years old, a plague of gypsy moth cater-pillars defoliates five million acres of trees across New England, including four oaks in our front yard. My dad, sadly, cuts them down with a chainsaw, and we spend weeks chopping them and piling the wood for fires. The following year, in a rare twist of history, the gypsy moths return. This time, they've already destroyed so many deciduous trees, even the evergreens become their target. My darling hemlock is eaten alive, one tree among thirteen million acres of forests from Maine to Maryland. I can't watch my dad and his friends take their chainsaw to her as well.

It doesn't make sense to cry for a tree, and it's not until I'm in my late forties that I grieve her.

I'm lying on the grass in silence at the Mwangaza retreat center, looking up at the clouds. My mind has finally quieted enough to let my body relax into the ground.

After a time, I roll onto my tummy and run my fingers over the clover leaves. I feel my belly breathing rhythmically against the earth, like a cat stretching on a patch of sunlight. My eyes light on the tiniest of flowers, only a couple of millimeters. It's intricate, delicate. I pick it and study it carefully. It's like a tiny orchid, no bigger than half my pinky fingernail. White petals, smooth and precise, dusted with sharp purple specks. The markings look deliberate, though they're no wider than a pin prick. The flower holds its shape perfectly, miniature and complete.

A tiny ant scurries over the petals, bustling in its urgency. I wonder if it notices the gorgeousness of its home. To the ant, does this enormous orchid, its petals wide and white, dotted with life-sized purple speckles, seem like an overwhelmingly beautiful place to live? Does the throat of the flower pull the ant in, with its deeper purple streaks leading toward the core, where five stately stamens stand? The bloom is hardy and upright, and the ant's weight is held easily on its porcelain surface.

Then I realize this mini bloom is one of thousands, maybe millions. I've been lying on them, crushing them, as I lounge on the grass. They're under me and surrounding me as far as the eye can see. Their minuscule beauty merges with the vast beauty of the skies. The ant is to the orchid as I am to this acacia tree.

There's immense beauty all around—and for whom? For this ant? For me? Just because? Some people might believe these mini orchids are weeds, ready to be mown. I see why my dad could never bear to cut down the bluets, tiny white flowers growing in our lawn, when I was a kid. He'd instructed me to carefully mow around them. The earth is filled with the glory of God as the waters cover the sea.

In a rush, I become a lily of the field. My body is filled with Presence. It's like love, but bigger. It's a complete filling and fullness of joy. I can no longer lie still, so I leap to my feet, hands stretched to the sky. My body is rooted to the soil, my arms are petals, my core is the stamen, and love is rushing from the heavens to the earth through me and back up again.

There's a thrumming sensation. Instead of fading, it grows. There aren't any words for it, but I hope there may be some kind of artwork to express it.

When I return home, my body still buzzes lightly. I bring my acrylics out to the back garden. I paint an enormous white lily of the field, filling the whole canvas and beyond. There's nothing large enough to express the feeling inside, and these acrylics don't begin to touch it.

Over the coming months, I will paint it a few more times—myself as a lily. I attempt to express it in words, but the humans around me aren't interested, which is understandable. I wouldn't have been interested either in my corporate days. And really, it's not a thing for words.

CHAPTER 5

OUTGROWING EXCLUSIVE BELIEF STRUCTURES

"There was a time before maps when pilgrims travelled by the stars."

Joyce Rupp

I can feel my mom's fear pulsing through our Toyota minivan as we approach my grandfather's house. We turn to slalom up his snowy driveway, the tires fighting to find traction in the steep gravel slope. Facing us, my mom says, "You may find your faith is tested here, kids. Be polite but stand firm. You don't have to believe everything someone else says. We can still love and pray for Grandpa, even if we don't agree with his lifestyle."

My father's dad and his girlfriend Kathy are looking out their picture windows. Seeing our approach, they rush out to greet us with warm hugs. As I squeeze out of the back seat into the snow, Grandpa bends to give me a full two-armed bear hug and looks into my eyes with excitement. "It's Christi Cracker! Good to see you!" I try to keep from beaming too broadly back at him. He's a Unitarian Universalist and therefore suspect.

Kathy is sparkly, effervescent, joyful, playful, artistic. She's barely taller than me, and rests an arm around my shoulders, inviting me inside, taking my coat, wondering if hot chocolate sounds like a nice treat. I'm drawn in by her perky blue eyes and zest for living. She's wearing a huge silver brooch with a laughing face that she's made in her workshop. Her thick, multi-colored hand-knit sweater engulfs her tiny frame.

We're barely in the house before she starts cooking up some fun. She takes me and Kathryn into her silver-working area and offers each of us a silver wire to play with. She and Grandpa share the philosophy that children learn by play, and that making something beautiful and useful with our hands is good for our souls. Kathryn and I are entranced as we use her welding materials. We twist and coil the silver into rings for each other. We carefully collect leftover bits of metal to be melted down for other projects.

Back upstairs, we show off our bedecked fingers. My grandfather's minimalist home feels simple and intentional, a space carved out of his own hands. He's designed the ceilings to rise two stories high, drawing the eye up to the open loft that overlooks the main room. Everything smells faintly of pine. He built the furniture, solid and unadorned, each piece planed smooth and polished only with oils. Light moves easily through the space, falling across his artwork on the walls: geometric patterns made with care, precise and rhythmic, the mark of a mind that loves order and beauty equally. The house is quiet, uncluttered.

Kathy fiercely enforces their one rule about food, "Eat all that you want, but no more than you want!" It feels daring to comply. If I've had enough, I can leave some bites on my plate, not worrying if they will be thrown away later. If I want another slice of pizza, I can grab one. If I don't want something, I'm encouraged to say, "No, thank you." Despite my mom's concerns, Kathy is clearly in charge here. If we want ice cream, we ask and receive. Can this be my rule? There's a lot of choosing what I want, which feels dangerous, and it seems to apply beyond food.

Kathy and Grandpa leave us with their brass chess set and some games. They've got a lot of work to do to complete all their art projects before they leave home to spend their summer season further east. All year, they design and create silver and gold jewelry, geometric artwork, custom wooden frames, and small, intricate wooden games. They live in a wildly liberal community from June until August, earning their year's income from the sale of their artwork to the heady intellectual crowd that gathers there for the summer.

The Chautauqua movement began in the late eighteen-hundreds to train Sunday school teachers at Chautauqua Lake. Founded on the idea that adults of either sex are capable of lifelong learning, the movement invited adults to continue learning and growing well into adulthood, with their literary, political, cultural, and scientific circles. The founder, John Vincent, a Methodist minister, designed their program to be different from other religious movements by including recreation, artwork, and theater, suggesting that life is a great teacher and that social justice issues are part of mature adult education. Over time, Chautauqua slid down the slippery slope into secularism, teaching courses on financial management and the dangers of the capitalist philosophies of competition and reward.

My grandpa explains to us kids that he used to be a Sunday-school teacher, but now he simply believes in the "Golden Rule," loving our neighbors as ourselves, working for a better world, searching for truth with an open mind, using reason to explore ideas, and that everyone has the right to choose their beliefs.

Grandpa and Kathy invite my parents to go out for an evening alone, practically pushing them out the door to have a romantic date. Once they're on their way, we settle in for the evening, and they bring out a pile of board games and card decks, including a Ouija board and tarot cards.

My mom flings the door open, exclaiming, "I've forgotten my purse!" Seeing us gathered in a circle, prepared to engage in Satanic practices, she bursts into tears. She pulls Kathy aside, and we hear her speaking in an angry stage whisper. "I leave you alone with my kids for one second, and you're already trying to convert them to your occult beliefs! I knew I couldn't trust you. Now put away that Ouija board and don't try to destroy my children's faith while we're out."

My curiosity is piqued, but the Ouija board and tarot cards are put back into the closet, and we're invited to choose among the other games. My grandfather asks, "I'd like to hear what you kids believe. Are you Christians because you choose it, or because it's the only thing you know?" We freeze and mumble about how we love Jesus. He and Kathy give one another sideways glances. He says, "That's fine. You can believe whatever you like. I'm just curious." Now I understand my mom's concern. We must stand firm.

Later that evening, he invites us to a game called "The Padrone." We four kids sit in a circle on the carpet, knees crossed, waiting for him to begin. He leans back in his chair, eyes twinkling, a cracker box on his lap. "I am the *Padrone*," he says in a thick Italian accent, drawing out the word like a secret title. We giggle, half-afraid, half-thrilled.

He surveys us with mock seriousness, deciding who will earn a cracker. "You, eh—you've been good today. Here's a cracker for Christi Cracker!" he says, handing one to me with a wink. The others protest, but he waves them off. "The Padrone decides!"

he declares. I bite into the cracker slowly, savoring the crunch, the taste of being chosen. He keeps the act going, voice booming and exaggerated, handing out crackers one by one— all of them to me. My siblings protest louder, but The Padrone has decided I'm the chosen one. I'm exhilarated.

The next morning, I emerge from my sleeping bag up in the loft and make my way downstairs to join Grandpa and Kathy as they enjoy their chicory beverage—they don't drink coffee. They're about to bundle up for their morning walk to the post office. It's about a mile each way, and my grandpa's PO Box is number one, as he was one of the town's first to choose. He never misses a day of this routine, stopping to chat with neighbors, and having a pancake breakfast at the Perkins restaurant across from the post office.

I decide to walk with them. At the restaurant, my grandpa sits across from me at the pine table, his hands flat on the smooth wood. Sunlight slants through the window. He explains that there's really no difference between him and the wood of the table. Each is mainly water. Each is carbon atoms.

"You know," he says, tapping the table, "this," tap, "and you," he points at my chest, "are made of the same things. One day, this table will be gone. So will I. But everything is energy. Nothing is destroyed. It just turns into something else. One day, I'll be a tree and you'll be a lake. I could be a table. You could be a watermelon. We all think we're the center of the universe, because that's the only perspective we could possibly have."

I sit still, my hand pressed flat against the pine. The wood is warm, alive in a way I hadn't noticed before.

"So," he says, his voice soft, "we're all part of the same thing. For a little while, we just get to be this. You get to be Christi Cracker. I like your spunk." I can feel my heart pumping with a scary feeling of awe.

As we drive from their house later that day, my mom says,

"I hope you kids weren't too destabilized by Grandpa's crazy ideas. Can you believe he used to be a Sunday school teacher? And now, he's basically nuts."

Out loud, I agree, "Yeah. How can you trust someone who doesn't know the difference between himself and the dining room table?"

I've been raised to believe that questioning religious beliefs outside of a narrow range is dangerous. It's a "slippery slope" that I can only imagine involves hurtling downward without control. At the bottom, I will surely die, either landing on something with sharp edges or into something darkly murky, and I wouldn't want to find out which.

But moving away from white American evangelicalism feels more like a long off-ramp by gentle degrees. The highway continues, while I find myself veering ever so slowly off into the open fields. Gone is the thick, black pavement that's well-marked and built for speed, efficiency, and direction. Gone are the lanes and staying in them. Gone are the maps and signs. Gone is the fluidity of moving in sync with thousands of others who've learned the same rules of the road.

Falling into universal love is an untethering. It's nuanced and involves losses and discoveries of all kinds—womanhood, country, culture, language, family, humanity. It's an open field. No lanes. No shoulder. No posted limits. Out here, I can walk or run or lie in the grass. I can turn in any direction and still be on the path. There's room for breath, for difference, for mystery. Nothing needs to match. Nothing needs to be justified. Everything belongs.

At first, it feels desperately lonely. I wonder if I'm the only human in this wilderness, surrounded by coyotes, the Milky Way overhead. I cry to the universe to give me one kindred spirit. Living on the campus of a theological school is not an obvious place to question everything.

In a visit to the United States, I walk a labyrinth in the garden of our friend Margot, who's entered a world of "contemplative spirituality." With her, I can speak freely of all I'm experiencing—the vastness of Love, the difficulty in living it in this human experience. She's not afraid. I'm not so alone. If there's one kindred spirit, there must be more.

The off-ramp is quiet. It curves from the rush of traffic almost before I realize I've taken it. The lines fade. The rumble of engines drops away behind me. The pavement narrows, then softens. The guardrail ends. No one around me even knows I've left, because my body is still here.

Sister Pat has opened worlds to me. She's a Christian, and a Catholic nun, but she invites me into a world of Somatic Experiencing™, introducing me to teachers like Peter Levine and Gabor Mate, and welcoming me to my body, my sensations, my breath. In an assembly hall outside of Nairobi, we lie on the floor with two hundred others to do "breathwork."

The carpet presses against my back. My hands rest on my ribs. I inhale. I'm not good at breathing. The facilitator gently rests a heavy weight on my abdomen, inviting me to see if I can raise it—he wants my breath moving lower than it has, and he asks me to feel it moving in long, steady waves. The air is thin at first, then wider. I follow it down, slow, steady. My jaw unclenches. My shoulders drop. My belly softens and becomes powerful.

I breathe again. Longer this time. My ribs expand into my palms. The exhale drains out of me. My nose goes numb, and my head spins. My spine settles. My face warms. Thoughts slide through but don't stay. I panic a little, but a woman comes by and gently places warm palms on the tops of my feet. Slowly, she covers me with a thick blanket, and I relax deeper into breathing.

I take another breath. Simple. Heavy. Real. My body feels like it is finally here. I can tell that I'm inside my body, and that it is just a small form while I'm expanding far beyond it. I'm fluid.

In this world, spirituality is less about studying scripture and believing creeds. It's about being alive in my body. Sister Pat tells me that her work is called "spiritual direction"—a misleading term, as it's highly practical and not directive. It's about the fullness of choice, and the experience of the movement of Spirit through the body.

A full year before she turns 70, Sister Pat prepares me for her departure from Kenya for retirement, gently reminding me I'll want a new spiritual director. I can also feel the inevitability of my family leaving Kenya, too. My work visa isn't being renewed without heavy bribes I'm unwilling to pay. My oldest child is nearing 18, and there will be no more visas for my kids as they become adults.

I decide that my next spiritual director will be in Europe, with someone who can walk me through my next major life transition—the ups and downs I know will come with leaving a whole world behind and joining another.

I choose someone with a Christian background and with the hope that my changing approach to spirituality might receive nurturing and attention. Our monthly sessions are a lifeline for me as we navigate more change and loss than I think my physical body can handle.

Her consistent, gentle presence is a balm until suddenly it's not. I meet her one day, in the eleventh month of our fifth one-year contract. With the precipitous drop in estrogen, progesterone, and serotonin during perimenopause, my body experiences a near-constant buzz. I'm too revved up to sleep, and too tired and irritable to maintain the docile feminine persona expected of me. I tell her of my experiences, and she asks me what my source of strength is.

After minutes of thought, I can feel the answer rising within me. My North Star is a firm connection with my values. My purpose is to create communities of grace—spaces where people can be loved and cherished beyond any need to believe certain things. If I hold firm to the values of love, strength, and radical acceptance, which I can find deep inside, I'll never go wrong. I know this truth more than anything, and I'm filled with wild freedom.

I can see disappointment in her eyes. I've said the wrong thing. The right answer was meant to be Jesus. She sighs. Suddenly, I know in my bones I've moved beyond what she can offer. I let her know the following week that I won't be renewing the contract with her after the next session.

Gentleness has its place, but I need space for the trouble-maker part of me—the wilder one who doesn't accept rote answers. The one who wants to build community based on the expansiveness of love that's within and all around and can't be contained by any one religion.

Tentatively, I reach out to Carol Kortsch. I've met her briefly, years before, through our friend Margot. Carol has owned a home and mini retreat center called Stonehaven in Philadelphia. I've been dreaming of hosting retreats since my little girlhood, when visiting my great aunt's retreat center. I'm fascinated to learn more about her work.

When I visit Carol's home, she brings out an enormous wooden bowl, gnarled and weathered. Carol's presence is elec-trifying, and I feel an instant connection with her, as if she's my long-lost great-grandmother. She's an ancestral figure, full of power that emanates from her tiny, lithe frame.

When she brings out the bowl and sets it silently in the center of the table, tears stream down my face. She's not surprised. She doesn't pretend to know what might be happening between us, but she takes my hand and shows me the lotus blooms in her garden, the massive boulders facing to the four compass points, and bramble-filled burial grounds by a stream that borders her property.

When I email her now from France, she invites me to her "Elder Soul" community. I'm not yet 50, and her hardy group of wilderness lovers averages in their seventies and eighties. But she assures me the Elder Soul is strong in me, despite my youth. These women are Muslim, atheist, Christians, Buddhists, and agnostic. They're bonded by having lived in multi-cultural environments, by their experiences of feminine power, and their love for mystical experiences in nature. I'm scared and enticed.

Carol assures me that there's a huge, wild world of goodness and love beyond the constraints of any one religion, and that all paths bring their share of goodness. She reminds me of Rumi—inviting me to meet her in the field beyond wrong-doing and right-doing. She speaks less of God, Jesus, and scripture—though she's intimately familiar with those worlds, having been born and raised in Angola and attended a mission boarding school in Zambia—and more of bones in the desert, fires built on high ridges and rocky outcrops, and the wildness of water.

Hers is a world of poetry and wonder. As a teacher, she assures me that knowing things is overrated. She cherishes mystery and confusion, insisting on teaching "at the edge and beyond my own learning." By speaking beyond her understanding, she invites us to join our wisdom with one another. With Carol, and the wild women we encounter, I can feel the last guardrails of highway-style religious living slipping away. The wilderness calls.

Our first Christmas in Alsace, France, my parents stay for a few days. My dad, true to form, plans far in advance, buying tickets in July, just before the two of them set off on a massive road trip across the United States to see every friend and relative they've missed seeing in America, while they were in Kenya for twenty years. His email is succinct and factual, as usual.

In those few days of their December visit, we drive up to Strasbourg to enjoy the famous outdoor Christmas markets. Chalet-style booths are set up on the Cathedral esplanade, offering mulled wine, toffee apples, Alsatian almond biscuits, bretzels, wooden toys, and hand-blown glass ornaments. With its cheery atmosphere, it's the perfect pick-me-up in a lonely year in a new place for our family.

My dad is as excited as I've ever seen him, showing me his favorite spots from when he travelled to this part of the world as a general manager for work. He takes us to his favorite *choucroute garnie* restaurant and is disappointed to find it closed. "Welp, I guess I'll have to take you back here in March. It's delicious and you'll love the ambiance. They have exposed beams and the softest-glowing lamps." We opt for paper plates of the Alsacian sauerkraut on the street instead.

He's thrilled to discover I have a *Daring Greatly*™ speaking engagement in Saint Gallen, Switzerland, during the ten days he'll be back in March. Pulling out a Swiss map, he traces our route. "I have so much to show you there! I can't wait to drive you across Switzerland and show you the Abbey in Saint Gallen. We could even go a little out of the way so you can see some of my favorite haunts in Liechtenstein." With his finger, he shows me. "One of my favorite train rides is to go east from Zurich toward Liechtenstein, then south and connect to a narrow gauge that goes up the Alps to Andermat. I'll take you to where I used to hike up and have a picnic. We'll have the perfect lunch of cheese, sausage, and a baguette."

Our last evening together, we sit around the dining room table chatting past dusk, as a light snow falls. They've got to leave at four in the morning to make their flight from Zurich, but we want to sneak in one last conversation. I pour out my woes of feeling misunderstood and alienated in the patriarchal version of the faith we've found ourselves in. We're all a bit nervous about the state of the world as Donald Trump has just been elected.

My dad, a life-long Republican who always voted straight down the ticket, despite living in a liberal state, expresses his disgust that so many American Christians have been duped into voting for such a man of obvious ill will. We never talked politics as a family when I was growing up, but I'm relieved to hear him speak so clearly. He sees the lack of integrity and maturity in tying hyper-capitalism and religion to one man who seems to flaunt his amoral views. Then he makes a statement that surprises me: "I hope I didn't waste my life defending evangelicalism." From my perspective, he always seemed far more likely to defend the scientific method and data-based inquiry.

He turns the subject to his usual favorite topic—theoretical physics—which my mom has often reminded him over the dinner table "is not of general interest." He's been reading about string theory, chaos theory, and quantum physics. Drawing on a napkin with his fountain pen, he creates wiggly lines like rubber bands, explaining that things aren't particles—they're all connected.

He grasps to find words to describe how, even though things appear haphazard, chaos has its own laws. His near-black eyes are twinkling as he describes the strange twists of energy throughout the universe, and how particles that are billions of light-years apart are part of the same string, so a tiny movement locally has more distant-reaching effects than we've ever imagined. I'm enthralled.

My mom jumps up from her seat in a panic. "I'm going outside!" she says in a strangled voice. "Honestly, sometimes I don't even know if you're a Christian anymore. You sound New

Age with all this talk. Those New Agers are always saying, 'Everything is energy. Everything is energy!'" She leaves the house into the cold air, slamming the door.

My dad, with his PhD in physics and twelve patents to his name, sits quietly and scratches his head. "Well, everything *is* energy."

When my mom returns, we give them final hugs and head upstairs to bed. Ben drives them to the airport in the darkest part of the night.

The time between their Christmas visit and their March return is tumultuous. I turn in a giant stack of paperwork to our local Italian consulate, the result of four years of rigorous efforts, in the hopes of gaining Italian citizenship. My dad and cousin have been helping me track down several generations of birth, marriage, and death certificates of our relatives, and my dad has brought me the final pieces at Christmas—his notarized birth and marriage certificates, apostilled and translated. My mom has gotten the stack translated into Italian. Unfortunately, the Italian consulate doesn't know how to process the paperwork for an American living in France, and they think I might need to go to Italy, so I've got more strategizing to do.

In the month preceding my parents' visit, we had also decided to announce we were leaving the organization we moved to France to work for. I had loved helping run their mother/daughter camps, encouraging moms to speak words of encouragement and connection to their girls, and designing creative activities to bring them together. They offer some beautiful couples work, helping people to bring tenderness and compassion into their relationships with grace and skill, and Ben and I listen to couples in difficulty during their retreats.

When we moved to France, the intention was for me to offer coaching to the organization's volunteers. I was excited to work with 150 French folks willing to give their time for more loving family relationships. But before I'm allowed to listen to them deeply and help them decide how they want to be most effective locally, I've got to learn the organization's counseling methodology. I find their method, which they call "biblical counseling," distasteful. I'm not only meant to use it, but to teach it.

I've already become a problem. In our first meeting with a patient, we're supposed to offer a form in which the person says how many times they attend church each month, whether they participate in occult practices such as yoga or using essential oils and which sins they engage in, such as homosexuality, pride, or gluttony. We interview them, listening for problems which we're to call their "sin patterns." Following the first meeting, using a medical model, we meet with a supervisor to offer a "biblical differential diagnosis," and scripture passages that will turn the patient from their wicked ways.

After coaching for ten years, there's no possibility I can treat another human being this way. In my coaching intake, I invite the person to answer open-ended questions about what they most love about themselves, their dreams for their lives, and how I can support them to remove any blocks on their way toward their goals. I'm listening for goodness, for health, for the strengths that will help them find their way to new joy. I normally call my clients my "conversation partners," not patients. They're experts in their own lives, and my role is to witness them in wonder. My main job is to be open-minded, encouraging the widest range of choice possible in their lives, and dealing with any of my own judgments that might get in the way.

But when I question my boss if the intake form sets the right tone, I'm seen as an insurrectionist. These forms have been developed by highly qualified medical doctors. Who am I to want changes?

When I see my first person, who I'm supposed to call my patient, instead of using the intake form I simply ask her what's bringing her in for a chat. As she speaks about the challenges in her family, I invite her to take some time in silence and to ask God directly for wisdom, however she understands God. When she does, she receives insight into how to set appropriate boundaries with her three adult sons and leaves our session with confidence.

The next day, instead of bringing my notes about her sin patterns to my supervisor, I'm called in for questioning for going off script as I seem to be some kind of wild woman gone rogue. How could this woman possibly have a direct connection with the divine? Is this some kind of witchcraft? I'm told I won't be seeing patients again.

My next foray into service goes no better. Some women from a local church invite me to lead a session with them, as there's been an enormous amount of infighting within their female leadership, and they need team building and to learn better communication. They're thinking that maybe doing some baking together will help.

Instead, I outline a proposal based on Brené Brown's *Daring Greatly* curriculum. The women are excited as we talk about how vulnerability, clarity of values, the seven elements of trust, and owning your whole story are some of the pillars of courage that are most effective in rebuilding relationships where trust is broken. What if the women were real with one another, and talked about the heart of the matter? They're pumped and invite me to lead the sessions, but first they need their (male) pastor's buy-in.

The following week, I receive a ten-page email from the pastor outlining why I'm heretical. To his credit, he purchased Brené's book, read it, and understood it before lambasting her with a lengthy two-column spreadsheet showing how each of her main points is in direct contradiction with scripture. The pastor wonders how I could have brought such a Trojan horse within the walls of their sanctified assembly. The women sheepishly inform me that I've been disinvited, and my boss is incensed that I've brought shame to their organization.

Once again, I'm in a system where women are devalued, honesty is suspect, and male headship is glorified while passive-aggressively undermined. I can't do it again. And rather than going to scripture as my guide, I find myself going to Saint Brené for strength.

Around a month after my parents leave for Nairobi, Ben and I let the organization we are seconded to know it's time for us to move on.

It's out of the frying pan and into the fire, though. We want to do our work as coaches and spiritual directors independently. But the policy of the organization that sent us to France insists we must be part of a team, so to leave our seconded organization we move somewhere else in France and join others who already work for our "sending organization."

We've always been well-loved in our sending organization and the missions organization we initially joined. It's an organization based on grace, as few policies and rules as possible, and open communication. Our colleagues in Kenya have been wise and wonderful, and we were given numerous opportunities to lead. So, we're sure that when we let our leadership know we're struggling, they'll be a supportive home base for us.

As it happens, between our arrival in France and our current situation, there's a new sheriff in town. An American man who has been brought in to lead the French branch of our sending organization. He's here because he's a "straight-shooter" who can help them sever ties with their local French counterparts. They need a rough rider to do the job.

He tells us that he's just like Trump—he doesn't have to be everyone's cup of tea, but he is the boss, and expects that when he asks people to jump, they'll want to know how high.

When he hears we're not aligned with our seconding organization, he's furious. He berates us for being unable to get along with the locals. He tells us to just go home, saying he has no place on his team for people pushing fifty. Plus, he wonders why I, a woman, am doing the work while Ben is driving the kids to school. Who wears the pants in our family anyway? "If a man can't be the missionary, what's he doing here?"

He decides our family needs to go through his new process, which he's developed cookie-cutter style for newcomers, who he anticipates will be twenty-somethings, like he was when he started in missions thirty years earlier. His process involves one year in each of four places, which means a move for our family every year. Our first stop will be language training. Next will be working with a team on an interim basis. The third year is an internship under a senior pastor. And the fourth year will be joining a team at our final settling place.

We've got three neurodivergent kids in an already tumultuous transition and this plan won't work. But he is a "Yes, Sir" kind of boss, so we agree to a trip to the first destination to research the French classes. We pack up our family and head south for the weekend to find what we suspected—the language school only accepts beginners who need to get to A2 or B1 level. Ben's French is already well beyond their top-class offerings, and my French is near-native fluency. They look at us like we're nuts and offer us private tutors but suggest we could also get a private tutor at home if we think we need better French.

Next, we talk with a couple on the opposite side of France, who work with refugees to give them language skills, health services, and access to jobs. They're a sweet couple with small kids and show us great kindness. They have their own ways of dealing with our new boss, using the "Gray Rock" method. They ignore him as much as possible, delay responding to his rants, and offer only the most minimal information in a monotone. We could see ourselves working with them, and it might mean fewer moves for our family, as we could skip directly to the fourth step.

We're reeling, and at the end of our rope. I've hardly slept from the mental whiplash and complete lack of support. I wake up on February 26, 2017, to an email from my mom to my siblings and me, telling us our dad was in the hospital following a heart attack. He was due to see the cardiologist in the morning, and they would decide whether to put in a stent or if he should have an angioplasty.

I call my mom to ask if I need to get a plane ticket, but she assures me that our grandpa had the same thing at that age, got a bypass surgery and lived another twenty years. No big deal.

My brother's family still lives near to my parents, and my sister-in-law swings wonderfully into action, setting up a family WhatsApp group and giving us the play-by-play when she visits Dad at the hospital, and he is put on a balloon pump. At 1 p.m. we get the message that his bypass is complete, and they are restarting his heart and will then close him back up.

Then nothing for hours, except that they're having trouble restarting his heart, until my sister-in-law calls. I begin to cry before I can even answer the phone. She tenderly says, "Christi, I'm so sorry." It's my job to call his only living family members— his sister and niece.

Our men are quiet, steady and quick. All three husbands pool their resources to get me and my two sisters plane tickets to Kenya on the same final flight through Schiphol in Amsterdam for the funeral. The plan was for my sisters to accompany my mom back to the States.

At the funeral home, I see his body, unclothed but draped with a red Maasai blanket. The funeral home staff have uncovered his head, and his hair is a little matted. He would have combed it neatly with the black comb he kept in his pocket-protector and kept my mom from being annoyed. But this time, she just sits quietly stroking his hair. His beard has its familiar swirl on his right cheek. I hadn't ever sat and contemplated that swirl before—it seems new as I sit so still, so close.

We eventually move as if in a dream to another room to look at coffins. The prices are ridiculous, my mom says. Eight hundred dollars for a box his body would be in for a couple of days before the cremation. Who would be conned by such a rip-off? My mom had just bought my dad a brand-new pair of black Bata shoes he never wore. Why should my dad wear them now, when they could be given to a person in need? He could be barefoot and no one would know.

It is decided we would drive across from the city mortuary to where we could get a coffin at a cheaper price. My brother has the sang-froid to brave the traffic and steps into the driver's seat of the Pajero.

Parking is scarce, but we find a space just in front of a gaggle of coffin salespeople. The police step up. This isn't a real parking space. If we want to stay, 200 shillings would be a good amount to make sure our car is kept safe. A brief moral quandary is resolved when I pass two 100-shilling bills into a discreetly held-out hand.

As all five of us bright white folk step into the glaring sun, the crowd of coffin-hawkers swoop in. "Mzungu! Mzungu! Best price. Come, follow me." I take charge, pointing definitively to one woman in the second row who has caught my eye. "We go to your shop." A bit random, but effective. The rest drop back, defeated, and we follow her into the bowels of the coffin shop earth. We must have descended three flights of stairs, past thousands of wooden boxes of all shapes and sizes.

Arriving at her shop, we see through the dim lighting the distinctions between the plain, pine boxes assembled with their nails on display to the high-end, polished varieties with little glass windows near the face, and dual-opening doors. Some have shiny gold handles and cloth interiors. How to balance ultra-cheap with only-the-best for my dad, who meant so much to the students and the faculty of his university? Who had meant so much to me.

The selection process is brief. Shiny, but not too shiny. Yes, the glass window. Yes, the top-half opening. (Who needs to know about bare feet?) I eye the length suspiciously. "It looks a little short. My dad was nearly six feet tall." I gesture with my hand above my head. A salesman rushes over and presses down on the top of my head to demonstrate. "It's perfect. We will just push his head down a bit. He will fit." Problem solved. The coffin shop ensures smooth delivery of our product to the funeral home down the street.

The day of the funeral arrives, and the family gathers for photos around our selected wooden box. I can't do it. I sit apart on the first pew to the far left. I don't want to look in the glass window. I don't want to know if someone has pressed down on his head so that he fits. I don't want to touch his hair or bend down for a kiss.

I want him to be full-sized, wearing shoes, combing his hair, content to stop for a coffee at The Mug in the shopping plaza. I want him standing up, where I can lean on his arm. I want him to be the one on the airplane to Zurich. Damn these coffin builders.

When we're back in Amsterdam, my mom, two sisters and I stand clinging to one another, inching along through security at Schiphol. Tears stream down the face of the woman behind us. She repeats softly, "I don't know why I'm crying! I'm just crying because you're crying."

Hands shaking, I place my carry-on, my jacket, and my Kindle in a bin. My mom does not want to let go. I'm about to pass through the metal detector, heading for France. The others will catch a US flight later. My mom's foot scoots a duffel bag across the polished concrete floor. Among her clothes is the small, wooden box holding my dad's ashes.

How can I get on that flight alone? I'm going back to a new country where I'm unknown and unloved. I have no friends. No job. No one to lean on, other than Ben, who's as shaken as I am, and three kids who are all struggling to stay afloat in a new language and culture, having left everything in their lives behind.

At home, if I can call it that, I try to keep the worst of my pain from the kids. I'm overwhelmed by grief. It's not a sadness or an emotion. I've never felt such lostness and confusion. It's deeply physical and utterly debilitating. I feel like an elephant is walking on my chest. I cannot breathe.

Night after night I try to stifle my sobs. I don't want the kids to hear the animal howling that wants to leave my throat. A week after I'm back in France, I tiptoe down the stairs and lie curled in a tight ball on the tiled floor of the living room, hugging my knees to my chest, as if grief could somehow be contained if I just hug myself hard enough.

I cry out silently, "Please, God, please! Just send me a friend. I need one person on this planet to remember me, to tell me they're thinking of me, to let me know I'll be okay."

In that moment, there's a "ping" from my laptop, which is open on the coffee table. "Thank you," I whisper. It is 4:06 a.m.

I open my email. There's a message from our missionary boss who heads up the ministry in France, and who's ordered us to go to language school. He reminds me of the deadline to get him our language report.

My stomach feels empty. This can't be happening. There's no "How are you?" No acknowledgment that the world has tilted. Just what's important to him. The words blur on the screen. Something hollow opens inside. My hands hover over the keyboard. I stare at the screen, disbelief turning to heat in my chest. I'm never speaking to this man again. The words, "What a complete asshole," spring, unsaid, into my mind.

But I'm still trying to be a good Christian, still trying to live by grace and composure. I take a breath and type, slowly, "Are you aware that my dad just died?" Then I sit, pulse thudding, watching the little blinking cursor. It's holding back everything I want to say.

He responds that he already emailed the prayer team when it happened last week and reiterates the urgency of the language report. I close the laptop lid.

CHAPTER 6

SHEDDING "SUCCESS"

*"As water takes whatever shape it is in,
So free may you be about who you become."*
John O'Donohue

In my childhood home, perfection is not optional. It is expected because it is righteous, and because my mom still needs to gain the approval of her mother. My parents make sure we are in church not only on Sunday morning, but Sunday evening, Wednesday night, and any other time the church doors are open. We sisters attend our church's version of the Scouts, and on Thursday nights we host a Bible study in our home.

My dad sleeps through most sermons, with much elbow-jabbing from my mom, but he does love to sing in the choir, directing and accompanying on his trumpet, and never misses Tuesday night choir rehearsals. My mom takes copious notes on the sermons and keeps a brush in her purse for the long trip up the center aisle to the church ladies' room for corporal punishment. For less visible squirming offenses, she can employ the less publicly humiliating in-pew skin twisting.

Both parents are heavily shaped by the teachings of Dr. James Dobson, known in the seventies for teaching parents to physically break the will of inherently sinful, disobedient children. Then for training them in purity culture and modest dress in young adulthood, culminating in virginal, heterosexual marriages without birth control, which allows parents to reproduce the system with a "quiverfull" of new soldiers for Christ.

The bathroom sink must be scrubbed with a toothbrush, every corner shining, because my mom, as God's special emissary, plans to stop by and check the grout. Homework must be finished by Saturday night, even if it's 11:59 p.m., because Sunday is The Lord's Day. Always. Monday mornings are a time to begin the week with all work complete.

I'm intensely motivated by gold stars. We keep a chart in the piano bench to mark our "accomplishments" and "initiatives." We get extra gold stars on the chart for completing additional chores. My siblings can't see the point of working for stickers, so their charts remain nearly empty, but mine goes on for page after page, as I come up with closet-organizing projects, extra deep cleaning chores, and anything I can think of to gain my mother's recognition and thanks.

Our food is excruciatingly simple and spare. We eat discounted day-old bread, or the dry brown loaves my mom bakes in the oven in a dozen tin coffee containers. We eat repetitive foods like fake Cheerios for breakfast, purchased in bulk bags with no cardboard packaging, plain mashed potatoes without seasoning, and overcooked chicken drumsticks with salt. I long for the processed snacks my friends bring to school, and sneak food from the pantries of the houses where I babysit.

Though I'm only a mediocre flute player, I practice daily so I can play in front of the church. My sisters' violin playing takes center stage in our home, as they have an exceptional set of teachers who have them perfecting each note using the Suzuki method, the most common pedagogical method used in homeschooling and Christian schools, in line with Bill Gothard's strict, performance-based philosophy.

Since there's no flute teacher at our school, and I'm not progressing well enough to be exceptional, oil painting is also on my schedule. My mom drives me each Saturday, over a couple of years, to meet with a wildly red-headed bohemian painting teacher, in the hopes I can be the family artist since I clearly won't be the family musician. I must have an area where I excel, so I am to round out the family's accomplishments with skillful representations of trees and flowers.

Family reunions on my mom's side are about performance, with the hope my mom could impress Grandma and receive longed-for accolades. "Come, show the aunts and uncles what you've been working on," my mom says, while I stand with my flute or give a speech, entertaining a crowd balancing potato salad on their knees. One of my older cousins jokingly tells me, "My mom says we're not doing the whole talent show thing, like your family does, because we're not that talented!"

Valedictorian of my high school class? It goes without saying. I have straight As in every subject since my earliest days, winning each year's reading contest, a book-reading marathon judged by my mother at our school. As my prize, I receive each year's Caldecott award-winning book for best illustration when I'm in elementary school, and the Newbery award winners for best literature when I'm in high school.

When I leave home for college, I have the humiliating experience of auditioning for their elite choir. Trained only in our podunk high school choir, I can't even begin to read the sight music, let alone sing in harmony with the professionals. My dad says his one regret is that I didn't join the chorale, not understanding that a child of his might try out and not make it.

I also audition for the drama club. I'm half in love with the elderly director who has kind and playful eyes. He's looking for the uninhibited. Following the instructions to move around the room like a lion or a snake fills me with discomfort, but I desperately want to loosen my body without fear. Then, we're sitting in a circle, the smell of sawdust and paint from half-finished sets filling the room. He leans forward, smiling, and asks each of us to name the body part we like most about ourselves. Laughter skips around the circle as people describe how they love their legs, their hands, their eyes. Someone even shows us their cute outie belly button. When it's my turn, my mouth goes dry. I stare at my lap, willing something to come. I can't think of a thing I like about my body, so I ask to pass. The director nods compassionately and moves on, but I feel the heat in my face. A week later, the list of drama students is posted. My name isn't on it.

Since I'm clearly not perfect, I decide to practice what it must be like to be carefree. Maybe by imitation, I can imagine what it must be like to be someone else—someone nonchalant, fun, and effortlessly cool and chill. A messy, playful person who's easy to love.

During that first semester at college, a group of us friends, who I can barely believe agree to be associated with a nerd like me, go to an improv club. The air buzzes with chatter, and my nose takes in the unfamiliar smell of beer. When the stage lights come up on three actors, one is already stumbling through the scene. He stops, stares at the audience, and blurts an absurd line about his below par performance. The crowd roars. My friends are doubled over, clutching their sides, tears streaming. I laugh too, because they are. I'm observing the scene as if I'm the actor, playing the part of having a hilarious time, while wondering how those on stage can submit themselves to messing up and making mistakes in front of everyone.

That same month, we try our hand at breaking and entering.

My hallmate is a lifeguard and has the key to the pool, which is off-limits after dark. It's midnight, and the place smells of chlorine. Breaking the rules has us giggling. Dim lights from the hallways flicker in the near darkness. We peel off our clothes, shoving each other toward the edge. I yell and leap in, making a splash that soaks the tiles. The sound bounces around the cavernous room. Everyone is shrieking, flinging water, wrestling in the shallows. I push my hair out of my face, shivering but laughing with them. The thrill is real, as is the thought: *What if we get caught?* My friend Peter remarks that girls have an advantage because of our built-in flotation devices, and I think, *Are we really talking out loud about boobs?*

Inside the vast hall with infinite choices that is the school cafeteria, I indulge in sixteen years' worth of contraband snacks. There are no limits on what I can eat once I've swiped my card at the entrance. After piling all the slices of deli meats and cheeses I could ever want onto a specialty rye bread, I turn to the soft-serve machine. It hums as I swirl the ice cream high in a bowl, adding gooey chocolate chip cookies on the side. I lick my spoon and laugh quietly. Everything is so delicious, satis-fying, and abundant. I'm nearly drowning in a sea of good food, and I gain thirty pounds, bringing me closer to the average weight of my friends.

At a party on our "brother floor" where the guys are separated on the opposite side of the dorm from the girls on my floor, the music is pounding. The girls I've been assigned to live with are naturally cool, and get invited to parties, so I coast along. One of the guys tries to light his farts with a cigarette lighter, while another, mercilessly teasing him about the disgusting state of his unwashed underwear, sets a pair on fire. The blaze earns them a $500 fine and a stern talking to by the fire department. Rather than end the party, they begin a goldfish-eating contest. I stand in the doorway with a red plastic cup of soda. Someone tries to tug me into the room, but I'm happy as an observer.

Before sunrise, the dorm is silent. I slip out of bed like clockwork at seven, and click on my desk lamp, careful not to wake my roommates. My books are spread out, notebooks open, highlighters ready. I sit, shoulders hunched, pen in hand, and dive in. I need to get in another hour of homework before starting work at eight and then taking more than a full day's course load. This is the part I don't tell anyone. While they sleep in, I'm making sure I keep my top scores, while working part-time to pay my share of the bills. If I work without wasting a moment from seven in the morning until six at night, I can graduate with honors, while still convincing everyone of my new, relaxed, fun persona. When I graduate magna cum laude, with more than a whole year's worth of extra credits, my friends are stunned.

I've been sending my resume to the HR department at our French headquarters regularly every few months for years. I'm determined to do an assignment in Paris.

I have wonderful memories of my student days there, of working in a restaurant in the elegant Passage Choiseul. The passage is a covered shopping arcade in Paris's 2nd arrondissement, the longest of many covered passages in the area. I recall emerging from the Quatre-Septembre metro stop and entering a hidden realm that's home to fashion boutiques, bookstores, jewelry shops, art galleries, and restaurants, just at the entrance to the Théâtre des Bouffes-Parisiens. After work, I would walk along the Rue des Petits Champs and sit in the open galleries at the Palais Royal to watch moms with children in strollers enjoying the pebbled walkways.

As a teenager, serving fresh-squeezed orange juice and

home-baked muffins in a tiny restaurant with only six tables is magical. The owner clearly thinks I'm gorgeous, and he has me customer-facing, shouting at me from time to time in heavily accented English, not because I need instruction, but because "it looks good to the locals." My unlucky male colleague is sent to the basement to *faire la plonge*, or scrub the dishes, a job that's never assigned to me.

I'm sure that if I can land another year in Paris with my wonderful husband, it will be just as magical. Still, when the letter arrives in 2002 inviting me to a new job at the corporate headquarters, it is a shock. I'm only three weeks into an executive MBA, when I'm invited to Paris to lead the employee stock purchase plan of our government-owned company that's about to be privatized in a historic move. I quit my MBA, reasoning that this opportunity will be like an on-the-job business degree, as I learn about mergers and acquisitions, IPOs, EBITDA, privatization, and other important-sounding finance terms.

It's early August, and I'm given only three weeks to join a high-powered group of professionals for a kick-off meeting with the Chief Financial Officer on August 28. I'll be the international communications person, responsible for internal communications and press relations. I'll be joined by a cross-functional team of representatives from legal, finance, HR, and other parts of the company. I'll be the only non-French member of the team, or in the whole building where I'll be working, so the pressure feels red-hot.

Ben and I go into motion at lightning speed. We find three single women from our church to rent our townhouse. I hire three people to replace me at work and still don't realize I might have been working too hard for too little pay. We pack a few possessions, mostly kid things, into large suitcases, sell or give away most of our furniture, and shove the rest of our personal items into the attic.

We're only torn because Ben's little sister has just announced she's planning to move near to us to attend Bible college. We're heavy-hearted to inform her we're leaving for my dream job instead of being there to welcome her to her new home.

We jump on a plane with little Micah in tow, their pack-and-play ready to unfold on the other side. Ben will care for them. He's received a visa with the ignominious stamp that says, *aucune activité*—meaning he won't be allowed to earn money. He takes on the challenge of being a stay-at-home dad in a country where that's not a thing. He's already finished the coursework for a second master's degree, but he still has a thesis to write to keep his brain occupied, and he'll be able to tell French friends that he's working on a master's when he senses that telling them he's an *homme au foyer* will invite ridicule.

Ben's mom is discombobulated. She sends a newsletter out once or twice a year to her church friends who support their missionary endeavors, and she wants to know what she should tell them about her eldest son's situation. Ben explains to her that we're moving to Paris because his wife has gotten a two-year contract for a big job that's exciting, and that he'll be home with the toddler. Confused, she says, "But what am I supposed to tell people?"

When we receive her newsletter at our new address in Paris, it says that Ben has decided to move his family to France for language learning while he completes his master's degree in biblical studies, implying we're on our way to the mission field, and that learning French is step one of Ben's plan to preach the gospel. My job is not mentioned.

Arriving in Paris, we find that the company has reserved a tiny hotel room for me, with only a single bed. I call my contact in HR, and he asks if I'm traveling with my *nounou*, which I assume is a nickname for my baby, or *nourisson*. I'm alarmed to be asked if I brought my child on this big move to a foreign country, but

I simply say yes. It turns out that *nounou* is a nanny, and the rumor spreads quickly that this uppity new American doesn't go anywhere without private, live-in help for her child.

But he moves quickly to place us in a one-bedroom apartment where we can open the door and step out onto the Esplanade des Invalides. Micah is immediately at home chasing pigeons just as they did in America. The Esplanade is a broad stretch of open green in central Paris, flanked by rows of manicured trees and wide gravel paths. At one end stands the Hôtel des Invalides with its golden dome catching the light, while the other side opens toward the Seine. People walk, sit on benches, or sprawl on the grass. The space holds all the glamour and romance of Paris, a place of symmetrical French design and elegance. This upscale location doesn't do me any favors at the office, where people whisper that soon they'll all be expected to speak English if foreigners keep inundating their ranks.

I sense things are a little odd on my first day in the new office. When the big meeting with the CFO happens on the 28th, it lacks the excitement I would expect from such a major undertaking. Even though senior bigwigs are gathered, I don't get the feeling that privatizing a global company of 70,000 people is the true agenda. After introductions and a brief description of the plans, everyone heads back to their current jobs, except me, who is entirely seconded to this project. I head awkwardly to my new office to twiddle my thumbs.

The communications department hosts a gala that first week, with a couple of hundred people in attendance. I stand near the edge of the room, watching. The tables are laid with small bites—tiny squares of bread topped with pink salmon, bowls of green olives shining with oil, platters of fine pastries lined neatly. Bottles of pale champagne wait to be poured. The voices move quickly, light and fast, impossible to catch. Everyone knows where to stand, how to greet one another with warm kisses, and how to flow into conversation. I keep my hands close, noticing the food more than the faces, and awkwardly pick up a sticky appetizer. Just then, I glance around and notice that no one else is eating. What are they waiting for? The Vice President sweeps into the room, shaking hands as he moves toward the microphone. Picking up the mic, he gestures toward me. "When Christi finishes licking her fingers, we'll get started." There's an eruption of laughter as my face flushes.

Meanwhile, Ben gets to work on the endless red tape, spending long days at the *préfecture* to get our visas approved. Micah plays in the waiting room and peeks from the narrow new stroller Ben's gotten to fit through the turnstiles of the Paris metro. Together, they explore the grocery stores and markets and create their daily routines.

Within six weeks, things become clear at the office. The French government, in an about-face, has decided our global company will not be privatized. The CFO must have known this announcement was coming when I arrived, thus the lack of interest in the project.

HR contacts me to thank me for my service and to send me back to the States—to my old life and my old job. I explain to them that there is no old life. My house is rented out under a two-year lease. There's no old job. A new team has been constituted to cover press relations, government affairs, and internal communications. I'll be in Paris for the duration of my two-year contract.

They give me a couple of days off while they sort out the options. In the end, they assign me to the financial information office, where I'll be charged with managing the publication of the company's annual report, first in English and then translated into French. I'll be meeting with the heads of each business unit to gather financial data and present it to the world on sleek pages with engaging graphics.

Despite my near-native French, my new boss is dead set against having an American on his team. He's younger than I am, wears a tailored navy suit, slim cut, the tie knotted just so. His shoes shine. His hair is neat, carefully managed, with a heavy blond lock he repeatedly flips back off his forehead. He stands straight, chin slightly lifted, speaking as if every word is certain. His eyes skim past people. The air around him carries the edge of someone who has been told too early he is his family's crown prince, and he believes it.

He doesn't trust me with the annual report, feeling my work will reflect poorly on his reputation, so he takes on my project, passing out micro-tasks in my direction. He doesn't allow me in the meetings with the heads of the business units, as he needs those connections for himself. And the annual report of a French company will certainly be written in French first, as always. He loves to call me into his office late in the evening to point out flaws in my work, to offer me a lecture on how many bullets should ideally be on each PowerPoint slide, or to lean back with his feet on his desk to tell me his musings about why he's a fantastic leader while I'll never be more than a manager.

He sends me as his emissary to meetings where I'm asked to pass messages I don't agree with and defend them against his political adversaries. The general consensus is that he's a ninny, and I struggle not to openly agree. As the months go on, he takes to surprising me in my tiny office, opening the conversation with swearing and cut downs. My secretary looks on with compassionate eyes and comforts me when he leaves the room.

As the months inch by, I sleep less every night. I can't keep my food down, so I don't eat much. I wake exhausted, my head heavy and stomach in a hard knot. My saving grace is that my company has merged with another group, and there's now another American in my universe. Emily is joyful, has tons of blond-streaked brown hair, loves making fondue with her partner, is a consummate professional, and is happy to privately slam the establishment with well-placed expletives. She introduces me to another American man, and the three of us quickly learn we're all on heavy antidepressants, which helps me feel it's not all just me.

Another saving grace is that I find myself pregnant. I'm wracked with guilt at being in such a miserable state just when the tiny person inside needs to be washed with all the warm hormones of a safe and happy mom. But I'm delighted I'll have a Parisian baby to join her big sibling. We had planned to have our kids two years apart, but the move across continents has added another year between them.

My first French doctor experience is surreal. My kind and wonderful French colleague recommends the doctor he and his wife had consulted after the loss of their first baby and says she's very compassionate. I can't quite feel that when, on my first visit, she begins, "Take off your clothes." I look around. *You mean, strip down right here at your desk, while you look on, fully clothed?* It seems that's the case. I stand in front of her naked. She looks at me up and down disapprovingly. "My goodness! You're completely deformed. I'm putting you on a three-day grapefruit-only diet." I decide to find someone else.

My new doctor is a man in his fifties who sits behind a large mahogany desk in a three-piece suit. The high walls of his office are covered with giant tableaux of nude women in various poses. I sit on a leather seat across from him, and he asks me to undress. "Do I take everything off?" I say. "That's what all the women ask me!" He roars with laughter at his own humor, and says, "Yes, please!" Somehow, I find his humor easier to stomach than the previous doctor's pointed criticisms.

In my seventh month, I head across town, taking two metros, and climb the steep hill and two flights of stairs to his office. He takes my blood pressure, looks at me in alarm, and says, "How did you get to my office—in a taxi?" I tell him my route, and he says, "Someone with blood pressure as low as yours shouldn't be able to get out of bed. I'm putting you on two months' *arrêt de travail*."

It's a stop-work order that's written in triplicate. I'm given one copy to send to insurance. He keeps one, sending the other to my office, with the reason for my stop-work blanked out. I learn that a doctor's orders are unquestionable. No one at my company is allowed to ask why I've gone. I am not allowed to enter my office, not even to pick up the plant on my desk. I will be paid my normal salary. The stop-work will take me through the delivery, whereupon I'll receive another three months paid leave.

In an instant, I receive five months of relief from my daily misery. This pregnancy thing is marvelous! Ben and I decide that a stop-work order is no reason to be unhappy or stay home. Six weeks before our baby is due, we purchase train tickets to Venice for our tenth anniversary. The train pulls in during a record-breaking heat wave. We step off, and the air smells faintly of salt and damp stone. The canal glints green, crowded with boats instead of cars. Colorful buildings rise from the water, and old walls stained with centuries of tide. Bridges arch every-where, narrow and worn smooth by feet. The twisting alleys sometimes open onto a square with a church or a café, some-times end at the water's edge. This is the land of my Italian ancestors, who were born, lived, and married just an hour north, toward the snow-topped Dolomites. Ben wanted our tenth anniversary to be epic, and it is.

A couple of weeks later, I have strange contractions. It's a Tuesday afternoon, and I walk from the lovely, high-ceilinged apartment we've moved to in Neuilly-sur-Seine to the Clinique Sainte-Isabelle. It's about a kilometer and a half walk, and I stop every few minutes to settle myself through the cramping. I'm assured by my midwife it's just Braxton-Hicks and to go home. I ask if I can be seen by the last of the three midwives at the clinic, so I can be sure to have met them all, as I know the baby will be born this week. They tell me it's sure to be at least another three weeks, and that the midwife won't have time to see me. I can feel the baby has dropped down low, and I know there's no way she's waiting more than another couple of days, so *j'insiste* in my most persuasive French to get an appointment for Friday morning.

I walk home, and on Thursday, the uncomfortable spasms begin again. I call my friend to stay with Micah, telling her the baby will be born that night. Again, I walk to the clinic, and again I'm turned back. This time, I insist I'm not going home. The nurses don't know what to do with my stubbornness, and argue vehemently that this baby is not coming. I argue equally vehemently, so they call my doctor. He says, "Always believe the mom. Even if the baby doesn't come, what's the harm in her getting a good night's sleep at the clinic?"

They offer me a bed and give me a medication to stop the contractions, since it's false labor. But it doesn't. They give me a second dose, sure the contractions will stop. They don't. So, they come with a needle of morphine to help me sleep. As they are about to jab my leg, I say, "Would you mind checking my dilation again, just in case?" They acquiesce. "Oh! You're four centimeters dilated. Good thing we checked, or it would have been too late to give you an epidural."

We head down a staircase, the contractions hard and fast now. The epidural is quick and painless, and they settle me onto a gurney. It's two in the morning, and I call Ben saying, "You'd better come. I'm sure I'll need you to hold my hand soon," thinking of the many hours of hard labor I'd had with Micah's birth. He arrives to find me sound asleep. At five on Friday morning, the third midwife, who I haven't met yet, wakes me with a smile and says, "You see this computer screen? I know you can't feel anything, but the next time you see this line go up, please give me a push."

She calls my doctor, who lives next door, and he arrives with a massive bedhead and puts on gloves. Not too sleepy to joke around, he shouts, "See this big plastic bucket?" setting it between my feet. "That's what I'm going to catch the baby in!" He roars with laughter. I give a small push, and there's our Leila, guided safely by his hands.

I'm treated like royalty for the next three days, pampered with massages and pedicures, and offered three-course meals cooked by an excellent chef. Nurses watch the baby each night while I sleep. When I check out, they regret to tell me I'll have to pay eleven euros, because not all the extras are covered by insurance.

I walk out with Leila in my arms, energetic, healthy, and ready to walk the thirty minutes back to our house where I'm allowed to relax and enjoy her company for four full months. From the first day, this kid enjoys sleeping without adult interference. She's calm and alert, taking in her surroundings with wide eyes, doing her best not to be squeezed too hard by her big sibling.

The next few months are everything Paris is meant to be. Micah goes back to their *école maternelle* after figuring out that babies are boring and just sleep all the time, and that they're in no danger of losing any of our love. Ben and I soak up the beauty of our apartment and all the delights the city of lights has to offer.

I can barely bear to return to work, leaving my beautiful kids for the long hours of meaninglessness and put-downs. I speak with HR, and they privately tell me, "You didn't hear this from us, but your boss is a known *connard*. We're surprised you lasted this long." Gee, thanks! I had been thinking I'm just exceptionally bad at cultural integration and office politics. They move me to another place in the communications department, this time with a kind and encouraging boss and team. I'm allowed to go home at more reasonable hours, and am widely accepted by my colleagues, though my work is still tedious and below my capabilities. HR is pleased with my contributions and delighted that with one American in a sea of two hundred French people, they now have an integrated, international office.

My colleagues enjoy my company, but I don't feel like they know me. At a restaurant in America, I'd be sitting at the center of the table, animatedly interacting with everyone all the way down to the end of the table, adding to the constant rise and fall of laughter and quick replies. I'd be gesturing with my fork, interrupting, catching a joke, and adding a quick comeback. I'd be funny and engaging, messy and warm, with the whole table bursting into laughter at my sharp wit.

Instead, I'm always shunted toward the end, or at a separate table, listening quietly to an introvert who tells me deep intimacies. I can feel myself changing. There's even a phrase for it, "expat introvert." It means that, in their home culture, they're naturally an extrovert, but in another culture, language barriers slow expression. So instead of thriving on quick banter and fluid social interactions, they lack the vocabulary, idioms, or cultural timing to keep up. So, there's a retreat into silence. Instead of being the life of the party, they become quiet observers because the rules of humor, storytelling, and body language shift. Normally recharged through socializing, in a foreign culture, everyday conversations can feel like work and cause an unusual craving for alone time.

I recognize myself in this description, not feeling quite myself, and missing the ease and flow I had, and feeling sad to be seen as shy or distant when that's not who I am. The extrovert in me isn't gone, it's muted. I'm learning to live with the introverted version of myself. It's fascinating because living in the "introvert space" is a different way of seeing the world. I observe patterns and behaviors more keenly from this quiet land, and my conversations become richer and slower. I listen more. I feel far more like my introverted husband, who's lived his whole life in other cultures.

Unfortunately, my anxiety and depressive symptoms return, not because anything is unbearable but the thought of entering the tall black tower and being in that high-stress environment makes my heart sink. And the toll of not being myself is more draining than I want to admit.

We're more than two years into our stay in Paris, and HR has offered me another two-year contract. I feel I should accept it. Life is good—the company is paying for our apartment, furniture, medical coverage, and utility bills, so we're socking away a huge portion of my six-figure salary, when we don't spend it on vacations. My husband is an active member of the Paris STUDs group (Spouses Traveling Under Duress) he helped found with a few other English-speaking stay-at-home dads. The kids love their play time on the Champ de Mars and their friends in their little school and daycare. Our friends would miss us if we left. It's probably okay if I'm not eating or sleeping, if everyone else is happy.

I decide to see Emily's therapist to help me cope. It's the kind of therapy where you literally lie on a comfy couch and the therapist guides you through a relaxing visualization before hearing the ills of the day. I describe my thoughts and feelings, my eating and sleeping patterns—or lack thereof. She's got me diagnosed with my usual acronyms, including major depressive disorder, generalized anxiety disorder, panic disorder, and OCD, none of which help me feel better. I pay her €200 each time and wonder if it's worth it.

When I tell her I've signed on for two more years with my company, she looks at me thoughtfully. "Hmm, I know everyone else is happy, but two years is a long time for you to be unhappy."

I sit upright. Is it? Whatever happened to muscling through? What happened to sacrifice, for loving others before oneself? For taking one for the team?

We are only halfway through the session, but I hand her the €200 and nearly bound away, my mind racing. I'm supposed to be happy. I had no idea.

I still haven't lost even one of the fifty pounds I gained during my final pregnancy, here in Kenya. These dratted hormones! Even though my youngest is almost two, I still think I look nine months pregnant. Our three kids are off to the local school, and I'm working as a volunteer in the budget-free communications office at a local university in an attempt to regain my identity as an adult who knows things.

Three years after leaving Paris, it's tough being a fat mom instead of a six-figure executive. A thirty-second floor office in a skyscraper in Paris, with a bougie gym and daycare center in the building is hard to give up for a two-bedroom, cockroach-infested, concrete student apartment with no office. Suits, heels, and makeup are things of the past.

No one here knows I led a continuous improvement program for a thousand communications professionals. No one has seen the comms strategies I developed for global messaging for a 70,000-strong international company. No one has an inkling I used to set up meetings with U.S. Vice President Dick Cheney, or that I saved my company thirty-two million dollars in one fell swoop, with a spark of genius to add a phrase to an international tariffs bill in Congress. I can't tell them, because it would seem like bragging, and it sounds ridiculous in this world, even to me. Who would care?

Here, people ask if I'll bake a cake for their wife's birthday. I lie on the grass with the other moms. I shop at the vegetable market on Wednesdays.

As a volunteer coordinator, I regain a little of my self-respect. I manage an office of student volunteers, training them in the basics of portrait photography, graphic design, messaging strategies for the university's main stakeholders—the donors, the alumni, the faculty, the students—setting up communication channels online for the first time, while still having brochures available for the rural population. I feel busy and valuable, if dramatically underpaid with a zero-dollar salary.

I settle into a four-month project designing this year's graduation magazine, the one major annual print publication that will sit on coffee tables all over Kenya and beyond for years to come as relatives brag about their loved ones' master's degrees. With no budget, the creativity needed to make something lovely fills me with a sense of challenge. In many ways, it's more exciting than working on a big corporate annual report with highly paid agencies at my command. This magazine is not a huge money-maker, but the advertisement revenues we've brought in will more than break even, and we've created a sleek, classy design that highlights the top students and offers each member of the campus community a voice. I pour my heart into it, and Ben is left many evenings watching the kids.

As the project nears completion and we're ready to print, a charismatic, broadly smiling white American dean with a doctorate in theology, comes back from his year in the States with a huge bag of donated flash disks, which are something of a novelty. Without talking with me or my team, he goes directly to the head of the university. They decide that our magazine won't be printed this year. Instead, we'll save money by putting a PDF of the document on these thumb drives and handing them to those attending graduation. Instead of seeing a photo of their relative on the page, they'll have this little USB gadget, though they have no access to laptops.

I see this dean on campus and stop to ask him about the logic of this idea and explain how our advertising contracts mean that we owe it to those who've paid us to print the number of copies they're expecting. He breezes by, baring a row of bright white teeth, and says with spite, "What do you know? Your job is to shut up and do what you're told."

A thunderstorm of emotions explodes somewhere deep inside. I can't speak, and I feel the familiar fog descend into my frozen core. The indignity is overwhelming. Every smart-aleck white Christian male authority figure in my past is wrapped up in the man strolling away from me. My feelings threaten to destroy my entire digestive system.

I grit my teeth and return home. I don't sleep a wink that night, my thoughts turning over the words I would love to speak and can't. I feel my inability to swear is a severe deficit. Angrily saying, "What the actual h*ck" lacks a punch, and boy, do I feel like punching someone. I cannot, I refuse to head into the pain that's a deadening of me.

On my third night of no sleep, I'm terrified of lapsing into one of my old depressions. At 37, I know the signs well. This is not a fun situation, but surely I'm adult enough to handle a little criticism. I do everything in my power to tame my ego and tame the sin of pride.

Ben says, "Okay, that comment was wrong, but this seems to have triggered something deeper. You need to sleep. Can I set up an appointment for you with Dr. Lee?"

Dr. Lee teaches a class on spiritual warfare. His specialty is forgiveness. He and his wife agree to see me privately in the small cottage behind their house for a two-hour session of healing prayer. Gently, he hints at stories from his childhood that led him to be furiously angry as an adult. He describes an angry bear with an arrow in its leg. While the problem may appear to be the bear's anger, the problem is the arrow. When you remove it and heal the wound, the bear can go back to its day.

As he listens to my recent run-in with the dean, he invites me to find "the arrow" behind the current anger. Where in my life have I felt this? My mind jumps to when I wanted so desperately to call the cops on my mom.

He takes me back to that kitchen, but this time he wants me to invite resources to help me speak the truth. He suggests that Jesus or the Holy Spirit can stand beside me and give me the power to speak up. In my imagination, they are there. He asks them to speak words of comfort, love, blessing, and truth to me. I can hear them say I'm lovable. I'm free. I'm strong. I'm meant to be here.

When I feel solid enough—powerful and loving—Jesus and I turn toward my mom, and I feel my powerful voice say, "Mom, what you're doing to me is wrong. Parents are meant to love their children, not hurt them. It's not okay, and I need it to stop. I am calling child protective services, because we need help."

Jesus is not rescuing me or doing the job for me. He's just beside me as I find the power within. He loves children, and he wants good things for both me and my mom.

I can look at my mom with compassion and love, powerful enough for her to hear my hurt and pain. She agrees to get our family help. Next, Dr. Lee invites me to look around the room to see what demons might be lurking. He explains that demons are just lies. While they seem larger than life and scary, they're craven scaredy-cats that can easily be sent away. I have plenty of power to send them away, so why not use it?

I look around and see a spirit of accusation, as well as spirits of rejection, disappointment, and fear. Accusation is wearing a dark hat. She is tall and speaks with a severe, high-pitched, scratchy voice. It's a voice I remember haunting my dreams as a young child. As I tell the demons to leave, she is the first to turn tail and jump into a large wooden box with secure steel fasteners. Rejection, disappointment, and fear, which look to me like dark, shadowy rats scurrying along the floor, follow her.

I close and lock the box and invite the Holy Spirit to make the strong box disappear forever. It vanishes instantly. I have a few prescription sleep aids in my pocket in case this weird prayer thing doesn't work. But it does. I'm free.

Before I leave Dr. Lee's cozy cottage, he turns his soft brown eyes toward me and speaks firmly, "Christi, you are a blessing. That's your true nature. That's who you are." My eyes fill with tears as I allow his words to seep into my heart.

After a good night's sleep, I walk into the office of the university president and show him the cost and revenue figures, explain the value of the printed magazine, and invite his opinion. He sees the sense in what I'm saying, thanks me for my efforts and for speaking up, and we go back to the original plan without much fuss.

I guess that's what's possible when accusation and rejection and their buddies are put in their place. And when my voice is filled with truth, power, and love.

Over time, I recognize the same physical feelings whenever the bad guys are lurking. Tight chest. Dizziness. Beating heart. No sound. I learn to pray for myself. To call upon love and power to join me in speaking the truth.

I'm grateful that soon after, I experience another disappointment. I'm on a search for a home and a place to be wanted and needed. I apply for a position hosting visitors at the campus guesthouse. My application is rejected, and I discover nefarious politics are at work.

Once, this would have sent me into a tailspin. Amazingly, my old demons don't return. I know without a doubt something better is in store. I am a blessing. That's my nature. I can contribute beautiful things to the world, which will be far better than anything I'm trying to grasp.

I do not strive for perfection. I do not fall into depression. I fall into a sense of love and protection. I sleep like a baby.

CHAPTER 7

THE CORNER OF LOVING STRENGTH

"Give back your heart to itself, to the stranger who has loved you all your life."

Derek Walcott

My big brother and his family have been living for twenty years in various countries in East Africa, but after a harrowing incident involving killer bees, they opt for the softer lifestyle of Kenya, where their kids are already in boarding school.

Upon their arrival, my mom warmly invites their kids to spend the weekend at their house. My brother's wife calls me, wanting to know if she can ask a few questions. I hesitantly agree before confirming that, yes, it is possible my mom might spank or discipline my nieces and nephew without my sister-in-law's permission. That Mom was also quite likely to leave her grand-children alone with the orphaned teenage boys she's found on the streets and with whom she has an open home. There are about a hundred of them who call her "Mom" and look to her to provide for their education and shelter while she fundraises for them. Yes, it is also very probable she might neglect to give her grandkids food.

My sister-in-law thanks me for my time and, in a clear voice, confirms her kids won't be going to Grandma's alone. She hangs up.

I sit in silence. You mean, it's that easy? You can just look at the facts and decide? I had always thought that you had to wait and hope and pray the worst doesn't happen and then agonize when it does. I hadn't realized I could set my boundaries based on data, not false hopes. I didn't have to tie myself in knots trying to figure out what to do, and how to say things sweetly enough not to anger anyone. Oh.

A month after working with Dr. Lee on forgiveness and securing the feelings of fear and rejection in a metaphorical lock box, I'm invited to join a circle of eight women from several countries across Africa. Suzanne, the Canadian coach who saw my tender heart after I was categorized as the only female D in the DISC personality test, is leading the activity. I am awed and enthralled by her stature, her business acumen, her composure, and her joy. She's the first woman entrepreneur I've met, and I'm inspired by her feminine leadership. She's everything I want to be— poised, professional, wise, and kind.

She tells us we'll have three questions, and that each of us will answer all three questions in turn. She doesn't say a word as we speak from our hearts, and instead maintains a huge container of nonjudgment. I'm amazed at how much I can express in her presence.

Question one is, "What do you want?" It feels edgy and dangerous. No one's asked me what I want before. It's so stark. What do I want about what? What about what everyone else wants? What about what everyone else thinks?

I'm the third person to speak, and I hear myself stuttering that I want to take a coach training class. In my twenties, I had taken a "What Color is Your Parachute" class with a guy from our church, and my assessment had shown I was meant to be a teacher or counselor. I knew I didn't want to design lesson plans or grade papers for little kids, or to spend my time listening to other people's problems. So, I dropped the idea and built my career in corporate communications.

However, in Paris, my friend Tracy took a coaching course. She offered me ten free sessions as part of her training. Even though she was a brand-new coach, I found myself making clear decisions with the process she had used. It was because of her, combined with my work with the therapist, that I knew I wanted to leave my job, rest, sell my house in America, and move to Kenya. Giant life changes came from being with someone who let me hear my own voice.

Since that experience with Tracy, I have been wondering if coaching could be what I've been waiting to find. It borrows the best strengths of teaching and counseling but transforms them into something fresh, collaborative, and empowering. Like a good teacher, my coach helped me learn. Like a skilled counselor, she listened with compassion and depth, but for possibilities, not problems. And, unlike either role, I experienced coaching as a true partnership. As the client, I was expected to be the expert in my life, a new experience for me. It's an enlivening process for both people—creative, and full of discovery. I knew coaching was powerful, but I didn't know if I was powerful enough to do it.

Now, with Suzanne seeing both my tender heart and leadership qualities, I think that, even if I don't deserve to be a coach, I can at least take a class in it. I've been looking at courses and mapping the budget and the timelines for months. Just saying it out loud is energizing and scary. And what Suzanne does is so elegantly simple. She asks a question and listens attentively. My thoughts race as the other women answer.

For round two, our question is, "What's holding you back?" This is obvious! When it's my turn, words rush out, "I know that if I try to become a coach, a voice will say, 'Who do you think you are to be giving anyone advice? You're such a complete basket-case, and I hope you're not setting yourself up as some kind of guru.'"

I stop, a red rush hitting my face. What a stupid, stupid reason to make decisions. Am I really going to allow a judgmental voice in my head to choose for me?

By the time Suzanne asks the third question, "What will you do next?" I am ready to run from the room and purchase that coaching course I've been drooling over for months, and I'm going to do it today!

If Tracy can be a coach, if Suzanne can be a coach, I can at least take a class. I strategize that, even if I never become one, I can at least use the learning in the service of others, and maybe become a better wife and mom.

I practically leap from my chair when we're dismissed, run home to our apartment, and open the tab on my laptop that's set to the page of the course I want. Getting out my credit card to make one of the biggest purchases of my life, I am stunned to find that the training provider is offering a fifty percent discount for purchasers in Africa this week, and that today's the last day to take advantage. I whoop in joy, convinced God's hand must be upon me and certain beyond all doubt that this is my next step. I join the course filled with anticipation.

A few months later in early August, my thirty-eighth birthday is approaching. My mom invites me to her home to celebrate.

Ben hotly protests, "Why do you want to ruin your birthday? Every time you see your mom, you feel like a comatose zombie for days. She brings you down. Why don't we just have fun with us this time?" But I don't want to upset her, so we pack up the kids and go as a family.

While we're at her house, she asks me to bring two chairs to the field so we can have a nice, long chat—the two of us, away from my "bratty" children who demand so much of my attention. My heart sinks, and I try to think of any way to get out of it, but she's insistent so I grab the chairs. My cheeks sag and arms droop as I prepare to listen to her bend my ear at length about all the annoying things my dad has done, how sneaky and untrustworthy her gardener is, and how badly behaved the social worker is she hired at her non-profit home for orphaned boys.

But I remind myself of the powerful forgiveness session I've just experienced with Dr. Lee, and that I'm a blessing. I take a deep breath and sit beside her in a folding camp chair.

Sure enough, she waxes on about a variety of complaints, but then surprises me. "What have you been up to?"

Taken aback, I offer the truth, "Well, I'm two weeks into a new life coach training course."

She sits up straight and stares at me, and bursts out laughing, "What do you mean? Who do you think you are to coach anybody about their life when you're such a basket case? I suppose you think you're some kind of guru who knows more than everyone else, as usual. Leave it to you to cook up an idea like that—always on your high horse!"

I sit in silence, with two trains of thought. The first is incredulity. The voice I had in my head when Suzanne asked what I wanted? Here it is—live and in the flesh—word for word what I had thought was my own inner critic. The second is to recall the forgiveness session, in which all the lies I've believed have been locked in a box and sent away. Here's one of those lies staring me in the face, and it's time to confront it with the truth: I'm neither a guru nor a basket case. I'm a person.

Grounding myself, I offer a quick prayer, "Holy Spirit, what is the next right thing to do?" I hear a nearly audible voice answer, "Ask her a coaching question." I almost rub my ears in surprise because the response is so quick and clear. It makes so much sense, though.

I turn to my mom and ask, "Well, if you had a coach, and you wanted something to be different about your life, what would it be?"

She considers. "I'd love to get back into playing the piano. And do artwork. You know, I almost never do anything fun anymore. I want to start enjoying myself..." And she talks for nearly an hour, with me offering the same non-judging presence I've seen Tracy and Suzanne use. I imagine she's someone I've never met; she's just another person I'm listening to about what she'd really like for herself.

When we finish the conversation with some next steps she commits to take, she's effusive, "This is the best conversation we've ever had! Were you just coaching me? You're the most amazing coach. I can't believe how wonderful I feel. I'm going to tell all my friends to come see you for coaching. It's so refreshing. You're the best coach in the world!"

Used to her wild pronouncements about how evil or gifted I am to her friends, I let her praises fall to the wayside. "Well, I'm only two weeks into the class, so I doubt I'm the best coach in the world yet, but I am really enjoying it and learning a lot."

When we rejoin the others in the house, Ben looks at me with surprise. "You look good! I don't think I've ever seen you come back looking so intact after a chat with your mom."

I'm surprised, too. This could be a new way of being in relationships. Not taking things personally, asking powerful questions, and letting the other person take responsibility for their own life, and me for mine.

THE CENTER

CHAPTER 8

MEETING DEATH, LIFE AND MY BODY

*"If you suddenly and unexpectedly feel joy, don't hesitate.
Give in to it."*

Mary Oliver

It's a dark, chilly Friday morning in January and I'm slowly recovering from my umpteenth bout of bronchitis. My sheets are in a knot on the floor from another restless night. My legs need to thrash. I kick the pile of sheets aside.

We've been married five years, and I've been alone in the house since Tuesday because Ben stays with our brother-in-law during the week while getting a master's about three hours from our house.

I don't eat but otherwise go through the motions of what needs doing to leave the house. It's time to go to work, and I never miss work. Hunched into my coat, I walk from our house on 7th along F Street toward the metro at Union Station. I'm gently crying, like I do most mornings these days. It feels more like a dark fog of nothing rather than a sadness. Tears flow down my cheeks, with no thoughts attached. My body is shrouded in a heavy veil, so I see the world dimly at a distance without feeling it. I'm vaguely annoyed at the cracks in the sidewalk I'm stumbling over.

Since my miscarriage a few months earlier, nothing matters. Not even the car speeding down 6th toward F. I step out into the road, directly in front of it.

The driver jerks the wheel sharply to the left, his tires squealing. He rolls down the right-hand window, and screams, "What the fuck? Get out of the road!"

I shrug. My body continues ambling across the road. It doesn't matter. I only wish he hadn't been able to stop in time.

I go into a dreamy reverie. If he had smashed his car fast into me, I could have been gone. Would it be like arriving in warm, soft, white clouds, or just nothing? Or, equally enticing, if he had only crashed into me at half speed, I might rest in a hospital for a few months, with white sheets and calm nurses. No more having to deal with friends dropping by or projects at work.

A few blocks later, my body trembles. Did I almost get hit by a car, sort of, but not quite on purpose? Is this really my response—to wish it had happened?

I sleepwalk through the workday, and when I get home, Ben's there. I tell him about the event of the morning. I tell him I think I need to get my hormones checked.

Ben's been taking a counseling class he's finding intensely interesting. He insists that I must see a therapist. Clearly, this post-miscarriage depression is not going away.

Saturday night, the restlessness is happening again. Nighttime is the worst, with daytime a close second. It's almost two in the morning, and my legs cannot stop moving and cramping. I roll off the bed onto the wooden floor. My fingers absently trace the splintered boards of our 100-year-old row house. Tears keep silently flowing, as I hold my flat tummy. If I can't keep a tiny, new life safe inside my body, what good am I? The universe is so vast, and I'm so helpless. Whatever I want, God wants the opposite. This body doesn't work. I don't want it anymore. God can have it back.

Ben wakes and hangs his arm off the side of the bed, letting his fingers run through my hair.

"Hey, sweetie," he whispers.

I don't want anyone touching me. I don't want anything.

He slips down to sit next to me on the floor. "Can I ask you something? Who is God to you?"

What a time to talk theology. Who the h*ck cares? I sit up next to him and think for a minute. My whole life, I've been taught God is the sovereign judge, the one who decides who's in and who's out, who's saved and who's tormented.

Ben sits quietly waiting. An image leaps into my mind. It's a deep, broad River of Life, and I tell Ben I think God is that river. Not a masculine figure ready to kill and destroy, but a source of everything needed for life. The river is there before me, as vivid in my imagination as anything I've ever seen.

Ben is confused by why I would be so scared and sad if I believed this. "Well, if God is a River of Life, what happens when you choose to take a drink?"

My breath comes in a sharp intake. What a thought! I could choose to drink? To him, it is a given that I, or anyone, could drink from this River of Life. For me, I don't believe it is an option for me to choose love. I was taught that God chooses, and I'm sure he hasn't chosen me. I know he chose Ben, everyone in my family, and all my friends. I've been hoping I can sneak into heaven by hiding behind Ben.

Suddenly, I'm rushing full speed toward the river, my body moving with complete abandon. I can feel my muscles pulsing and an enormous well of joy rushing through me. But just before I get to the river, my doubts resurface. What if something terrible happens? What if I'm not allowed?

I hear a deep, resonant voice up and to my left. "Of course I chose you. I love you. Go ahead and drink."

I realize I have never experienced deep down that love is for me. Not like this. The truth hits me: "Of course I'm chosen, too! Of course, all I have to do is accept and receive love! That is my choice."

I fling my body on the grass by the riverbank, laughing. I plunge both hands cupped into the deeply rushing stream, scooping cold water with ecstasy. It runs down my wrists, pouring back into the current. I gulp quickly. There's no possibility of selfishness because the sheer flood of water is so abundant. The cold hits my teeth, floods my throat, and I swallow hard, again and again, scooping and splashing. It tastes alive, fresh, like heaven pouring into me. My chest fills with laughter as the water spills down my chin, soaking my shirt, and still I drink, grinning at the wild joy of it.

I'm flooded with relief. I realize how hard it's been to do all the right things. To work so hard to pray, be hospitable, be helpful and loving, hiding all the time that I am an outcast. It's crystal clear to me I don't have to do anything at all except receive.

I fall into a deep sleep, full of joy. The next morning, we go to church, and I look the same on the outside. I'm doing the same things. I'm still a nice person, but it feels light. I feel like a huge burden has just rolled off.

Up front, our pastor is totally rocking out on his flute while his wife invites all of us, including me, to sing, "Don't you want to be a part of the Kingdom? There's so much love in the Kingdom. There's so much peace in the Kingdom. There's so much joy in the Kingdom. Come on, everybody!"

Now, I'm crying because the song makes sense. I'm not just

vocalizing it. I'm part of it.

A week later, Ben sends a note to some of our closest friends and neighbors, who've been worrying about me, "As her husband and the human who loves her most, I am excited about the growth and maturity I am seeing in her spiritually, emotionally, intellectually, and professionally. I'm very proud of her and feel like a new day is dawning in her life in more ways than one."

For one of the activities in my spiritual direction course, which I take over two years of retreats with Jesuit priests, we're asked to fold a giant piece of paper into quarters. Each quarter represents twenty years of our lives, assuming we'll be granted about eighty. For each quarter, we draw or describe our imagination of God. The idea is that our imagination will change over time, which goes against anything I've been taught. God is meant to be unchangeable yesterday, today, and forever.

But I realize the masculine, punishing, abusive, exclusionary God of my childhood, who's an anthropomorphized judge, father, king, or ruler has already been replaced. For now, in the final year of my 20-40 quadrant of life, God can't be a man. They're a pulsing plural, beyond gender, and an abundant, inviting River of Life, big enough to include me and everyone else. So, I let myself imagine what might be next.

Is God the same as Love? Is God all light? What if God is bigger, wilder, and more expansive than a river? What if God includes everything in an enormous, universal magnificence? What if everything is included, not just the warm, unconditional, tenderly accepting version of love? But the fierce thunderstorms on Lake Superior, and billions of galaxies whirling and expanding at lightning speed? Might I experience that God in my forties to sixties?

And what's after that? How could I even guess what the divine might be in my eighties? When I see 80-something women, they have such a wondrous twinkle in their eyes, as though those eyes were a pure channel of the laughter that is God's grace. They seem to know what matters, and it's not about criticizing anyone.

Maybe by then it just feels like God is springing up from within? That you feel completely part of it all, like everything that has ever existed is passing through you, and you're passing through all that is. Momentary and eternal all at once. It's just a glimmer I can't quite grasp.

What I do know, in a swift moment of realization, is that hell, a place of separation and eternal conscious torment, cannot be real. The River of Life would never design such a place.

Although I had certainly been living in a hell of my own making when I believed that a judgmental God was in charge, I am sure of one thing—every single person, including myself, deserves to hear a loving, compassionate voice. Deserves to belong. Deserves infinite outpourings of kindness.

It drops like another shoe that, if there's no hell, the only thing left is Love. Loving myself and others, with all our faults, will be the work of a lifetime.

Once I hang my fluffy red robe on the hook by the door, I am naked.

Everyone is naked, their bodies varied. People of all ages, shapes, and sizes have all come for a day of spa treatments in Bad Bellingen, Germany, about a half hour from my home in France. Legend has it that "SPA" is an acronym from the Latin *Sanitas Per Aquam*, which translates to "health through water."

The nudity is practical and non-sexual. Some women are here with close girlfriends. Some with a male counterpart. No one stares. My body is not so different from the variety of bodies in the room. Though surrounded by people, I am deeply alone. It's 2017, and just a couple of months since my dad's death.

People observe one another with the same interest they would if they were fully clothed, walking down a German street. Their focus is on the process: moving from heat to cold, from water to rest. The shared nudity is an equalizer.

I step into the first room, and the air hits my skin—warm, close, quiet. No swimsuit. No towel wrapped tight. A stack of handcloths rests by the door. Each person spreads a tiny cloth onto the tiled steps before sitting.

I feel the rough cloth under the skin of my thighs. I'm just me, bare, among other bare bodies. I don't know anything about where the woman next to me works, lives, or how she spends her days. I only know that she has a body. I try not to tense the soft, drooping fold of the tummy that has housed three babies. My tummy is okay.

After some minutes, I stand. I try not to shrink, but to stand tall as I walk to the next room, the next small towel to sit on, the next temperature—this one significantly warmer. As I sit in this warmth, I hear the words of Christ chanting like a refrain in my mind, "This is my body. This is my body."

My body feels uniquely mine, and also infinite. I spread my fingers gently and wonder at them. None of their cells existed seven years ago. Yet somehow the universe has decided that these fingers, this hand, will continue to be created day after day, mostly out of thin air. One day, the air that sustains me now will no longer enter my lungs, and these fingers will no longer be created in this form.

The heat rises as I move into the sauna. Wood under my feet. A hiss of steam. People sitting with their eyes closed, legs loose, arms open. I take a spot on the lower bench, feeling the wooden slats beneath the hand towel. My skin prickles. Sweat beads fast. Grabbing a glass, I swallow a long draught of cold water, feeling it move through my insides in sharp contrast with the warmth. I feel the chill settle into my stomach and gradually join my body temperature.

I remember my dad's body from a few weeks before. Hot tears spill down my cheeks as I'm brought back to the table where he lies motionless in the funeral home, covered with a red Maasai shuka. I can see the swirl of hairs of his beard on his right cheek. Breath no longer moves through his body. It's just a body now. But it was my dad's body, the body that created me, the body that used to be so warm as I leaned against it on the couch, the body I loved.

Shaking off the tears, I move to the hot tub. Six adults share this intimate space. The man next to me is kissing the woman beside him. Her legs are crossed over his, and her toes brush my knee. His thigh touches mine from time to time. Each of us will take it in turn to rise from the heat and walk across to the cold plunge pool.

My turn in the plunge pool is next. I climb the ladder in full view and drop into the shoulder-height wooden cylinder. Cold shocks up my legs, grabs my ribs. I gasp. The water closes around me, and the world contracts to one tight, electric moment. The cold pool is a solo experience. But my body, tingling with life, is visible to the half dozen men and women seated in the hot tub as I emerge. The voice repeating, "This is my body," fills with power and clarity. It's my voice.

At the end of the circuit there is an exfoliation massage. First, I stand to be blasted with jets of high-powered water up and down my skin. Then, I lie on a tiled table where a brisk, heavyset woman uses an enormous brush, which looks like it's meant to scrub down a garage, to roughly turn liquid soap into a thick foam as she moves it in large circles over every inch of me. Thankfully, the bristles are softer than they look.

As the outside of me is intensely stimulated, the inside melts into grief. I sob, letting out a keening cry that surprises me. My torso twists and curls, as my diaphragm lifts. My vocal cords try to expand to let in more air, while the muscles of my throat contract to swallow. As my lungs seek their freedom, the muscles between each of my ribs tighten and strain, causing a deep physical aching in the chest wall. Each muscle is fighting its partner.

The German woman stops scrubbing and shouts out words that remind me of a World War II documentary. Swiftly, three German colleagues rush over to inspect me, and ask staccato questions. I just want to be alone with my body, with my tears, but all I can say is, "English, please? *Ou français?"*

A French woman joins the melee. Speaking with infinite gentleness, she asks me in French what's wrong. Her brown eyes are warm and kind. I let her know in French I'm okay. I just need a good cry. The massage has stirred up the release of some much-needed grief. My dad has died, and I'm just coming out of the shock. She takes firm control, shouting at the Germans to leave the room, and they instantly comply.

She rinses me methodically and wraps me in the softest, warmest blanket. Leading me by the hand like a child, she walks me to the VIP relaxation room, which I haven't paid for, and which is beautifully decorated with nature scenes. She helps settle me onto a lounger and tells me, "Trust your body. And cry all you like."

This is my body. I am not dust. I am not water. I'm what happens when dust and water meet. I feel every speck of myself—inside and out—alive. To be here, in this vessel, right now, is the world's most wondrous miracle.

I'm floating spread-eagle in my inflatable hot tub, gazing upward toward the clouds, the water temperature just warmer than my skin. I had met The Minotaur and a part of me died. I had slayed my dragons in the center and could live from joy and peace. Everything about me feels smooth and liquid. My eyes close, and the water could be a whole lake.

A fleeting memory rushes behind my eyelids, of running home from the local pond with my sister, laughing through a summer rainstorm. The image comes with the sensation of being loved, being part of love, being an ocean.

As I merge with the warmth of the water, I feel sharp pricks of cold on my arms, legs, and face. The clouds above are dropping swift downward dashes. My eyes spring open, my face just at the pool's surface, and I observe the waters above connecting with the waters below.

Each falling bead breaks the liquid's skin, causing a momentary depression. As hundreds of round drops contact the surface, smaller droplets spring from the impact zones, the water in the pool responding to the water from the sky, creating an intricate ballet. The height of each rebound is commensurate with the size of the droplet, so the dance is vibrant with a variety of vertical leaps.

The sheer playfulness and the shock of the coolness send me into a peal of laughter. Now I know why babies are always laughing. This place is amazing!

In two minutes, this eternal moment is gone, the bright sun shining forth again. But the ripples of joy remain in my heart. I don't want to waste another moment, when joy can be lived once, then expressed, then shared again.

Joy, like all the emotions, is only meant to rush through the body in a minute. It can't be grasped or captured any more than a wave on the beach. But it can be remembered, deepened, and focused. It can become part of the communal wealth of life force energy, stored like an internal battery, for when strength and kindness are called for.

THE RETURN

CHAPTER 9

TUNING INTO MYSELF

"If you listen, you will hear what your heart would Love to say."
John O'Donohue

The most annoying love ballad in the French language, in my humble opinion, is by Jacques Brel. He repeats, *ne me quitte pas, ne me quitte pas...* don't leave me. He promises to become his lover's shadow, the shadow of her shadow, the shadow of her hand, even the shadow of her dog. And of course, she leaves him, because who is in love with their dog's shadow?

One of the ways I lose myself is by showing extreme devotion and loyalty, a willingness to sacrifice my needs and putting others on a pedestal. These repetitive patterns, which I recognize in myself since my earliest days, happen with friendships, work relationships, and in my family. I think, "If only I show this person how much I care, surely they'll respond."

The difficult truth is that the more I want to pour love toward others, the further they pull away. What people want is not constant availability and kindness, wonderful as those traits may be, if they're fraught with the unspoken expectation that the person then owes me their undying loyalty and will be forced to stick around. That sounds more like the cult-like relationships familiar to me from childhood. The more accommodating I am, the more the other devalues me. People aren't looking for a servant. They're looking for an equal adult, with the spark of contrast and uniqueness.

I learn that what gives people confidence in our relationship is a sense of inner strength and independence. We don't love people who plead, "I'll do anything for you." Our hearts are drawn to those whose presence tells us that they know who they are, what they stand for, and are just fine. Saying, "I love you, and I'm not willing to do that," is a beautiful way to build trust.

My counselor in my twenties told the story of someone who loves steak and is desperate for a perfectly barbecued chunk of red meat. So, she goes out to a sushi restaurant, even though she hates sushi, and demands a steak, waving her credit card in the air. The restaurant owner lets her know that no steak is available. They do, however, offer an abundance of delicious temaki, sashimi, and nigiri. No matter how she pleads and cries and begs, steak is not available. That doesn't mean there's any lack of steak in the world—as we speak, millions of cows are being raised for that purpose. So, why keep going to the sushi place?

If the relationship is a match, wonderful! If not, everyone will still be fine. There's plenty of love in the world. After a lifetime of fawning, pleasing, and giving, in the hopes of getting safety, belonging, and love, this new way of living feels terrifying and wrong. Walking away. Letting go.

One person who embodies this strong, fierce love is a woman I meet in Brené Brown's training course to become a Certified *Dare to Lead*™ Facilitator and Certified *Daring Way*™ Facilitator. Jacqui Sjenitzer shocks me from the start, inviting forty-five of us across Europe and Africa to join a group of facilitators.

I assume she's the leader of something, but she's just like me—a woman who's been through the training and wants to connect with others. Since no one else is creating that space, she's doing it. Furthermore, when I see her website and social media posts, she's brazenly wearing a t-shirt that says, "I'm the boss of me," while pointing to herself.

Her energy is attractive; I give her a call. She is generous yet boundaried with her time, open and authentic. She helps me with one of our first videos at Awaken Coach Institute, teaching about emotions. Later, I become her guinea pig as she tries techniques she's learning in her Somatic Experiencing® course, Peter Levine's trauma-healing methodology. With her, I learn to listen to and recognize my body's signals, to trust them, to move with them.

This concept of choosing myself and letting others come and go is difficult to grasp because love includes care, kindness, giving, and consistency. Long-term bonding depends on daily acts of devotion. Yet, someone who lacks passion for their own goals and makes others the center of their world loses their soul. With Jacqui, I experience a beautiful embodiment of what this kind of centered, boundaried, interconnected love and care is like.

I learn that, when I feel rejected by others, the most common cause is that I've already rejected myself. No one can or should fulfill my self-worth for me. I am the only one who can take responsibility for my life, freedom, desires, and choices. The more I become "the boss of me," the easier it is to receive and give love.

The source of healthy human interdependence is found in finding my healthy center and staying there. As my Aunt Vicki Joy would say to her dog, and to her own soul, "Stay... Stay."

The more I find my healthier core, the one that knows without a doubt I can be no better or worse than any other person, the more my demeanor changes. I'm more grounded, humorous, creative, and calm. When there's nothing to prove, there's a whole lot of clarity.

Relational therapist Terry Real says that the question to ask in any relationship is, "Am I getting enough from this relationship to make grieving what I'm not getting worth my while?" If not, it's time to grieve and let go. But how many times do I stay around, begging for a proverbial steak, when it's simply not what's on offer?

Terry Real also warns of the opposite danger, of becoming cold or emotionally walled off, which has rarely been my style. True strength lies in staying grounded in that healthy center, where I move toward situations and people where I'm naturally welcomed and loved, and stop pouring effort into unreciprocated relationships, or relationships where we're constantly trying to out-serve one another.

I know I'll be okay even if plenty of people don't like me, my leadership style, or my annoying habits. It's hard, though. I do love applause, and I find getting rejected difficult. A therapist I've been following for years, Jay Reid, brings a compassionate perspective on my difficulties. When we meet, instead of asking, "What's wrong with you?" He asks, "What have you been through?" He gently nudges me to stop asking, "How can I get someone to choose me?" and start asking, "Do I choose them?"

Rejection loses a large part of its sting when I check inside myself and ask, "Am I enjoying this relationship? Is this something I want? How do I feel when I'm with this person?" Strangely, sometimes the people I'm most desperate to convince that I'm worthwhile are those I don't feel good around. As soon as I notice that my body is saying, "You feel diminished in this person's presence," I can more easily let them go.

I decide to walk the Camino de Santiago, starting from Porto, for my fiftieth birthday. My body is in chronic pain, but I know I need to walk off some grief, lostness, and loneliness. Maybe walking will help me find my center again.

At lunch one day, a fellow pilgrim asks why I am walking the Camino. I have no idea, but a flood of words comes anyway. Multiple generations of mental health disorders in my family, mixed with a punitive religiosity, and a firm and consistent minimizing or outright contradiction of my lived experiences, along with my decades of wandering the earth, have left me questioning my grip on reality and any sense of where home might be. Who is the committee? Who gets to decide which stories are true? Who takes care of me when things get painful?

After days of walking, I am still searching for my center and my pace becomes humiliating. I am literally at zero percentile. No person on the entire Camino walks more slowly. Not the 70-somethings, not the people heavier than me, not the people with debilitating blisters or a broken foot. Perhaps I am uniquely defective.

I pack slowly one morning, making sure my sleep apnea machine, the heaviest and bulkiest item in the pack, is nestled at the bottom. The mist shrouding the steep walk down the cobble-stone streets toward my walking buddy Carol's hostel muffles my back and leg pain, and seems like a portent of something mysterious.

Arriving at a beachside cafe, I find Carol with her new friend Steffen, both sipping espressos. Expecting nothing more than small talk, I am completely unprepared for the bombshell that ensues. When I inquire where Steffen (a classically drop-dead gorgeous, athletic, muscular, self-assured, successful German man half my age) will be walking to that day, he responds nonchalantly, "I'm taking a rest day."

I look up for a lightning bolt to strike. *Who* on God's good earth has given him permission to do such a thing? And does that mean that taking a rest day is a thing? People do that? They just rest? Where's the committee that decides? Despite the progress I've made, I can still treat even self-exploration and pilgrimages with my former "push through pain" approach when left unchecked.

"Yeah, good idea. I'm thinking of taking a rest day, too." This is a lie; resting never crossed my mind. "What's up?"

He replies as if he's speaking common sense, "Yeah, I've got some inflammation in my knee from an old virus. I'm just going to stay here at the beach for a couple of days and take ibuprofen until I feel good enough to walk again." And that's it.

I realize I still don't make my decisions based on what I feel. To me, it's important to say that whatever hurts doesn't really hurt. To mistrust what feels good.

I buy my usual nuts and fruit supplies from inside the cafe, and Carol and I walk on as if nothing happened. But a seed is planted. Am I allowed to choose what I want, based on what my body says? Am I the committee?

On the last day of my Camino, I find that the center is inside me. A peppy young walker asks what I am proving by walking the Camino. "Proving?" I think he must be joking. What could I need to prove? After a miscarriage, a traumatic delivery, three live births followed by years of breastfeeding, losses of loved ones young and old, multiple global transitions, brushes with mortality, becoming my own CEO, and filling reams of government-required paperwork on several continents, "proving" anything seems ludicrous.

I tell him instead that I'm letting go. To protect my tender heart, I'm dropping my need to be an expert about anything, to be better or worse than anyone. I'm dropping the need to be tough and to show that nobody can hurt me. Dropping the need to find a home in America. Dropping the otherness and rejection that's dogged me all my life. Dropping the need to be the lightning rod for my family's anger and anxieties. Dropping the need for distance and separation. Dropping my desire to be loved and understood by people who aren't interested, and instead receiving the goodness from those who are.

CHAPTER 10

BROACHING BOUNDARIES

"Anything or anyone that does not bring you alive is too small for you."
David Whyte

The screen glows faintly blue as a short video by Jay Reid comes across my YouTube feed one Friday afternoon in 2020. The title is, "Altruistic Narcissists: Beware their Care." I can feel my confusion. How can narcissism be wrapped up in caring for others? It's my first time hearing about altruistic narcissists. I thought narcissists wanted to be seen as wealthy and beautiful, which is the opposite of my parents, who want to be seen as poor and self-sacrificing.

I never would have associated narcissism with giving, but as I watch the video several times, each sentence drops into my gut with a ring of truth.

Being able to trust that it's safe to receive love, to be given to, is hard for me. My mom set herself up as the greatest caregiver on earth. More sacrificial than anyone. There's the expectation that I, as a recipient of her care, will reflect how amazingly generous and kind she is, with profound displays of gratitude. The word "gratitude" makes me a bit queasy.

I think back to my high school days, when displays outside of the home of how much she cares for me are dramatic—she's publicly sacrificing by going to school every day with her kids, taking a job where she can be with us every minute. She's gone above and beyond by driving me to art lessons, music lessons, and drama class. It feels like pressure to be the best at each of these, display my work publicly, get the lead role, receive awards and scholarships, and thank my mom for how she's bent over backward for me.

Why doesn't it feel safe to receive love from her? It feels like I need to be a basket case, needy, and clingy to receive love. But it also feels like I need to be "the best" to show that all her efforts are worthwhile. I feel an internal split as I try to be both evil and good—hiding each side of myself from the other. I feel the need to tell people at school that my mom is the most generous person I know, which feels like truth and a lie. I wonder what would happen if I became successful without her input, as far from home as possible.

When I move to Kenya, I can see she truly is an exceptional caregiver. She's taken in so many boys off the streets that my dad gets fed up and tells her when he comes home from work, he can't be tripping on people sleeping on the floor. She'll have to build a real home and hire social workers for these boys if she wants to continue. So, she does. She fundraises for hundreds of street children in Kenya who might have died without her, catering for their school fees, clothes, and basic needs. It's incredible. So why do I feel so proud of her, so jealous, and so bereft? All the motherly affection I've wished for is poured out freely on so many others. She seems to have a limitless capacity to listen to these boys, to comfort them, and to cry with them.

For her sixtieth birthday, I buy my mom an incredible surprise. It's something she's wanted for ages, described to me in detail, and told me often what it would mean to her to be able to get to the orphanage and to bring the boys to their rural homes in remote areas. I plot for months to find a red Rav4, her dream car. I have to order it and have it delivered to Kenya from Japan, have it inspected and registered, washed, and ready for the day of her big party.

I'm imitating her generosity to a tee. I feel an intense need to help and to support her in her mission. I want to be sure my gift will be dramatic, with an audience. She'll never be able to say I didn't love and support her. See? Look at me, being beyond generous!

The last major gift I have given her was a quiet $10,000 to purchase a two-acre plot of land to build the boys a home when I first arrived in Kenya in 2005 from France. I never receive a thank-you, and when I let her know a note or a card would be appreciated, she responds, "Why should I thank you? Ten thousand dollars is nothing to rich people like you. I don't see why you are always grasping for thanks. It's not like you've sacrificed anything."

With this car, though, there's sure to be a big hug and a public thank-you. With more than sixty boys looking on, I offer her a box the size of toothpicks. In it are the keys to the Rav4. She opens it, and her jaw drops. "What is this?" she exclaims, looking around at the crowd. My heart bursting with love for her and pride at my surprise, I bring her out to the driveway where her car waits.

She gasps. "Boys! Can you believe it? Who wants to go for a spin?" She jumps in the driver's seat and calls four of the boys to join her. Off they drive in a cloud of dust. My dad and I go back into the house to finish serving cake and snacks. My heart shrinks as I fight back tears. No hug. No thank you. Nothing will ever get me the love I crave.

Soon after, she drives the Rav4 through a deep river in a herculean effort to save some boys during a storm, destroying the car's engine. She goes back to fundraising for a new car, preferably something with better suspension and more powerful than a Rav4.

So, now, watching this video on YouTube about altruistic narcissists, my breath stops. The words on the page dissolve. I see my mom's face. Her sacrifices, her endless giving. The silent invoice that always follows. The exhaustion she wears like a crown. It isn't just kindness, it's this. There's a physical drop in my stomach. A lock clicks open. *Oh.*

It comes with enormous turmoil, though. Everyone seems to want to label their parents as narcissists. The word is flung around so often, it seems meaningless. And I'm not sure labeling another person with the latest trendy disease will help. I research altruistic narcissism, though, and the pieces come together. I don't need to blame or label her to make things easier. But it does help me learn how to take responsibility for my healing.

Narcissism, I learn, is at its core a sense of emptiness and unworthiness. It's so painful to feel the shame that the outward defense takes on its opposite pretense of extreme goodness that's superhuman. I see myself in it, too. My desperate urge to help. My desire to fix my mom, through listening, gifts, coaching. If I can just be kind enough to her, she'll be healed. When she's healed, I'll be okay.

I learn that leaving the narcissist is the healthiest option. For someone who's been scapegoated, gaslit, and disbelieved, it can be important to walk away. I'm not ready, though. Leaving my mom, whom I've always believed I would care for in her old age, feels like I'd be ripping the core of myself out of my heart.

And what's more, I can feel the altruistic and the narcissistic traits in myself. The certainty that I know what's best for others. The surge of pride when my "help" works. It's not only empathy, it's grandiosity. The way I rush in to fix, to soothe, to give more than was asked for. The secret glow of being needed. It's me, standing in the center of someone else's story. I recognize how I, too, make my family members small so I can be seen as the one who's strong enough, good enough, to offer solutions.

My wounding keeps me from accepting even the mildest criticisms. Words intended to provide me with clarity and information can cut me to the core—even while I pretend to invite it. No one sees the flow of tears I hide after I've taken a dose of constructive feedback. Any small comment feels like an assault. It's not feedback; it's a denial of my basic goodness.

My chest is heavy, my breathing shallow. I look away from the screen for a long time. There's grief in seeing it clearly—how my giving has sometimes been a way to control, to avoid my help-lessness. But there's also relief. If I can name it, maybe I can lay it down. Maybe love doesn't need to be proven through sacri-fice. I am not afraid of the work. I am afraid of the part of me that wants the applause. The part that needs to be the savior or cult leader. The part this video names. The part I see in my mother, and in myself.

After my dad dies in 2017, the dynamics in my family of origin become more exposed, and the former constellation of relation-ships shift. There is now no buffer between me and my mom, and it's unclear who will take on the role of enabling her bound-ary-free behaviors, with her judgments and opinions, on others. I don't want the job. My mom goes to live with my sister Kathryn for nearly six months, which is followed not long after by the breakdown of Kathryn's marriage.

Now that my mom is alone, I find myself filled once again with compassion for her, and all she's suffered. I visit her in America, and she sobs as we walk together along the beach. It's a deep, keening sob that overwhelms me. Feigning strength, I hold her close and ask how she's doing, grieving the loss of my dad. She says, "I'm not crying for him. I'm grieving the loss of *my* dad for the first time." Her voice breaks, as she cries, "Why couldn't God heal my dad?"

I have no answers. I have been asking God the same question—why can't he heal my mom? She's gone more than fifty years without support for her losses. She counts on me to hold them for her. She's been telling me in graphic detail about her dad's suicide attempts since I was 12. His death when she was 19, and her unprocessed grief, have been hanging over me since I can recall. I long for her to have anyone else to talk to—a friend or counselor.

At a snail's pace, I let it sink in that my compassion is being misdirected. At least a sizable chunk of my compassion must be directed toward myself. No matter how much I love her, she is the only one who can get help for her grief, take ownership of her behavior, and give herself love. My job is to take care of healing my soul.

I am only responsible for me. If I want to love my husband and kids well, I need to hold myself at the distance at which I can love both myself and my mom. And that's a pretty far distance because whenever I'm with her, I'm hurting.

In 2020, as the world is closing during Covid, during the same week my sister Kathryn's divorce is being finalized, she suffers a psychotic episode, which ends up in her being hospitalized with powerfully inappropriate psychiatric drugs for a long period. The frightening hospitalization during Covid throws all of us into a tailspin. Kathryn's so heavily drugged, I'm not sure she'll survive.

I'm terrified because Kathryn and my dad were the two family members who showed me love in my childhood. There were a couple of movies that my family watched when I was little that haunt me—*Children of the Corn* and *The Bad Seed*. In both, psychopathic children murder their parents. The joke in my family is that I am the bad seed, I am a child of the corn. I am voted most likely to kill the rest of the family in their sleep. The other family joke, repeated regularly, is that I'm the "Girl with the Curl," from the classic nursery rhyme, with an emphasis on the line, "when she was bad, she was *horrid*." I believed that to my core, and I honestly feared when I was a child that I would become a murderer.

By middle school, I had become a violent, angry person. I hit my little sisters regularly. At 10, I stabbed a classmate named David in the head with a mechanical pencil. His mom had to dig the lead out. At 12, I slammed a girl in my class into the metal tampon dispenser in the girls' bathroom. At 14, I beat up a 13-year-old kid I was "babysitting" (why was I babysitting someone a year younger?) and locked him out of his house when he refused to obey my orders. Once, after I had been severely punished at home, I held a lighter to some clothes in my closet, toying with the idea of lighting the place on fire, starting with myself.

Through it all, I always felt like my dad loved and believed in me. His eyes shone when he looked at me. He showed me without words that he thought I was strong, like when he piled my arms high with wood from the forest to build a fire at home. He thought I was brilliant, which I learned as he sat by me while I did my math homework, using the Socratic method to show me I could figure it out on my own. He was the anchor of peace and security in my life. He thought I was beautiful, much to my mom's jealousy, comparing me favorably to each of his favorite actresses, no matter how little I resembled them. To him, I was

Sandra Bullock, Sigourney Weaver, Debra Winger, Kirstie Alley, and Jodie Foster all rolled into one. With my dad's death, I feel I can no longer survive the family's story of me as violent, horrible, and evil. I can no longer find compassion for them. It's too much.

Without him, and with my sister in the hospital while I'm on the other side of the world, I feel desperately lost. Everyone in my family of origin has so much good intent toward one another, and none of us has any idea who we are. In our world, where we're all meant to bring people "into the sheepfold" of our religion, and where there's a deeply-rooted fear of punishment and hell, we're trained to cross people's boundaries consistently. We delve into their thoughts, feelings, and beliefs in a well-meaning attempt to fix, save, and heal them. When a family member is doing badly, everyone tries to help, to offer solutions, to give advice.

My stance, hard won through years of coach training, of allowing others to make their own choices, even when I disagree with them, is considered wrong. I'm meant to be agreeing with the good guys and fixing and changing the bad ones. But there aren't any bad guys—just humans who've been raised without knowing how precious we are, and where one person stops and the other starts.

In the aftermath of my sister's hospitalization and her recovery, there's a volley of family emails that goes round and round with no boundaries, everyone offering opinions on everyone else's life choices. It's Kathryn's response to my mom that impresses me most. She says what I wish I had the guts to say:

"In spiritual direction, the number one lesson is that thinking you know what is right for someone else is 'trespassing on their sacred ground.' Each person is a unique representation of God, and discernment is so deeply personal that it is extremely

hurtful to the process to try and step in and advise. It only causes pain. If you want me to feel safe talking to you about any aspect of my life, you are simply going to have to stop lecturing. It was really nice of you to invite us to dinner and spend time with us. Then it was quite hurtful to immediately get an email making it clear that you aren't interested in listening to me, but just want to tell me your opinions and perceptions. I don't feel like explaining to you every detail of my finances, goals, and plans. So, I am not responding to the rest of the email.

I talk to my therapist once a week and Christi several times a week. Those are my safe people because they are helping me know what I want as opposed to telling me what I should do and getting their own opinions in the way. Hopefully, our family can learn some good listening skills."

My Boundaries Bootcamp coach, Molly Davis Moon, recommends Ben and I read Pia Mellody's book, *Facing Codependence*. Like me, Molly doesn't like to label people, so she doesn't diagnose me as a "co-dependent." Instead, she describes me as deeply compassionate with little recognition of my true boundaries, a.k.a. my true worth. I appreciate her warm description, which rings true, and makes looking at co-dependency more palatable. She reminds me that, without boundaries, our compassion often runs away with us, causing us to remain in harm's way far longer than we need to be.

Ben orders the book and the accompanying workbook for us both, and I open to the first page, which describes my experience exactly. Mellody lays out how, when the protective denial of what happened in childhood starts to fail, and reality hits home, the co-dependent realizes the sheer scope of the problem. Suddenly, the adaptive strategies deeply ingrained since childhood are overwhelmingly devastating, and progress seems to move slowly.

In a parenthetical remark on the workbook's first page,

Mellody makes a comment that shakes me. "Being functional (acting in your own best interest) feels awful, shameful, as if you are doing something wrong. But..."

I stop reading. Wait, did she just say that being a functional adult means *acting in your own best interest*? And she puts it in parentheses as if everyone already knows that's what being functional means?

I read the sentence several times. This does feel awful, shameful, and wrong. My head knows somehow that she's right, but my body screams that I'm supposed to be serving others! Isn't that what being a functional adult is about? Functional adults look out for the needy in faraway lands and ensure that their spouses and kids do the same.

Acting in your own best interest sounds like greed, selfishness, and capitalism. It sounds like the dreaded "looking out for number one" that I've been taught to despise. My judgmental self starts kicking me for taking so long to wake up. How many abuses have I suffered because of my lack of ability to stand up for myself? I live out of a helplessness learned in childhood long after I'm a fully-formed adult. How many times do I rush to ensure people can easily, smoothly take advantage of me financially, physically, sexually? How many times am I quick to reject and abandon myself, giving away far more than is healthy in friendship and business?

I struggle to find compassion for myself, and I am comforted to read that "Conducting life in the disease feels normal to a codependent." It does feel normal to give to others, and it also feels normal to be filled with resentment and emptiness.

I'm reminded of the supposedly beautiful story called *The Gifts of the Magi* my parents would read to us on Christmas Eve. In the tale, two members of a young, impoverished couple sacrifice their most prized possession to buy a gift for the other. The wife sells her long hair to buy a platinum chain for her husband's watch, while the husband sells his watch to buy expensive combs for his wife's hair. When they exchange gifts, they discover their sacrifices have made the gifts unusable, leading to a poignant and bittersweet moment that highlights the depth of their love and selflessness.

This classic story is meant to illustrate the true meaning of love. Love equals sacrifice. Love is a duty to others. In my family's view, you don't have to like someone or have warm, fuzzy feelings; you just have to do the right thing. And the right thing is giving away more than you have.

My heart now opens to new possibilities. What if the husband and wife communicate their desires to one another, and work as a team to gather the resources for one another's goals? What if, instead of silently giving and serving to no purpose, they act as equals, and can say freely to each other what they want?

Not recognizing my own infinite worth creates harm. My continuous sacrifices are part of an inadvertently destructive system of trying to out-give the other person so I can subtly control their behavior. Only knowing myself as valuable, treating myself as completely equal—neither more grandiose nor more shameful than any other—will provide freedom and health.

I'm tempted to pound myself with loathing and disgust. How can I be so ignorant of what makes a healthy life? I'm a coach trainer! I teach on boundaries. I was known for years as "the forgiveness coach."

I feel deep inside that the only way to truly love others is to offer unconditional love to myself, while also taking full responsibility, not blame, for my actions. It's almost impossible to have an equal, healthy relationship with someone who thinks badly of herself, finds herself unworthy, powerless, or helpless, and who is stuck blaming herself and others, instead of seeing clearly her responsibilities, which are to herself. I've found that out repeatedly in friendships, business relationships, and at home.

This boundary-crossing way of living is reinforced in hierarchical structures that operate with rewards and punishments, which discourage questioning authority or dissent. The boundaries work is more about feeling myself inside, getting to know my wants and needs. I used to think setting boundaries was mainly about setting limits on the behaviors of others, and being selfish. Now, I'm slowly sensing that it's much more fluid, and based on love radiating outwards.

Healthy living requires me to know my preferences, desires, loves, dislikes, red flags, and non-negotiables. And then to be able to express them clearly and without emotional drama to those around me. Expressing desires, fears, and wants is a daily, even moment-by-moment practice. Healthy boundaries look like being alive and attentive, and taking good care of my body, mind, and spirit.

I learn that healthy boundaries often sound less like "No" and more like "I'm not sure I'll want to go out on Saturday night. I'll pencil it in and let you know by Saturday morning how I'm feeling. Does that work for you?" Or "I'm getting that report printed on Friday. If I don't hear your comments by Thursday, it will be printed without them."

Hmm, that doesn't sound that hard, with practice. It doesn't sound mean. It just sounds clear, honest, a little vulnerable. And it sure beats making up stories about how rude other people are when they can't read my mind and therefore my silent objections. I practice saying what I want and need, even if I still can't bring myself to voice my pet peeves or dislikes.

I hope my body and mind will continue getting stronger and more dynamic. But what's most important is to embody love. I want my kids and their kids to know from each moment with me that they are marvelous, valued and important, and I can see how wonderful they are.

I want everyone who spends time with me to know they are

more than okay—they are designed to be a blessing. That is who I am, and it couldn't be otherwise. The more boundaried I am, the more I know the truth of my innate lovability.

In May of 2021, my mom and Ben have an email exchange in which Ben sets some boundaries around finances. My mom says she wants a closer relationship with our family and to support us financially, with some strings attached. In his email, Ben describes the reasons why he's unwilling, citing abusive situations that I and our kids have lived through at her hand.

In her email she responds that I was a good, helpful girl at times but like the little girl with curl, when I was bad, I was horrid. She continues that those times had taken their toll, and she had tried hard to get along with me and to help me develop my talents and grades. She went on to state that I had never apologized to her for driving her to the brink with my bad behavior as a kid. And that what is defined as abuse these days wasn't considered abuse in her day, nor is current parenting a happy medium.

I'm heartbroken that, even as I'm about to turn 50, my mom is still justifying and minimizing her behavior and wishing for an apology from someone who was a little kid when the abuses (which are not abuse according to her) happened. In her story, I remain the girl with the curl, instead of myself.

Therefore, after walking the Camino for my fiftieth birthday, I finally decide to go low contact with my mom. All the years of compassion for her have damaged me. It's time to turn my heart of compassion toward myself. And to turn my love and attention toward my husband and kids, without constantly wondering when the next drama from my family of origin will arise.

It's time for my mom to seek compassion for herself, if she so chooses, and to find wise counselors. Instead of allowing her to pour her heart out to me, I let go of trying to heal her. At home, I write to her briefly to let her know I won't be in email,

WhatsApp, or phone contact until she chooses to be in regular, consistent counseling. My message is simple and brief and easier than I had anticipated. My mom doesn't respond.

I don't hear from her again until almost a year later. I can breathe. I can feel my body settle, strengthen, and heal with each month that passes. The threat of drama leaves my home in France, and we settle into a new ability to see one another.

In June 2022, I'm starting a big, new challenge. Awaken Coach Institute is in its second year, and I'm thrilled with the beautiful impact we're having with each of our cohorts of participants, who are making amazing community and connections with one another. There's such a wellspring of love, and I feel like I'm getting the hang of leadership, community-building, running a business, and being part of good things. This month, I'm testing my bravest venture yet: we're going to facilitate our entire course in-person for the first time in a two-week retreat in Spain.

We've been organizing it for months. It's not only the most thoughtfully planned, prayed-over course ever, but a lot feels at stake for me. I've invested enormous amounts of time, love, and soul into creating the content, and put my heart out there for months on social media to fill the course. Everyone who knows me is sending me loving notes and warm thoughts for the big day.

The day of the retreat arrives, and I'm filled with every emotion as Basia Goodwin and I welcome the participants to her home in Castrillo de los Polvazares.

At Castrillo, on the Camino de Santiago, the path shifts. The dirt and gravel are gone, and the world becomes stone. The village is a river of large, round cobblestones that are a deep orange, from the road to the houses along it. These are not neat pavers. These are ancient, uneven, ankle-turning stones. The heavy green doors of the houses mark the turning point on the

Camino journey. Here, a pilgrim is leaving the emotional part of the journey and arriving at the plateau that represents the spiritual path. The village is a meditation space that forces a halt. The easy rhythm of the *Meseta* is shattered. This place is a threshold. There is no way to walk through this town and remain in your head.

As each participant arrives, tears flow. They've each said yes to a threshold moment in their lives. And they're counting on me and the Awaken team to hold the container for transformation. In my turn, I'm leaning on the River of Life, an ocean of love, and all the wisdom of the universe to support us. We begin with Basia and her husband Bertrand offering a simple, beautiful meal, and opening our retreat with a fireside poem called "Dusk," saying a quiet meditation in support of each other's pilgrimage.

I return to my room and open my laptop, making sure I've got everything prepared for the following day. There's an email from my mom to my whole family. I wonder if she's decided to encourage me on this big day in my life, as I know she follows Awaken's Facebook account.

Instead, she ignores what's happening to me. She's chosen today to write a lengthy "apology" for her parenting. She has not received any counseling, my prerequisite for her contacting me again, and instead makes a plea for forgiveness. She states that her desire to have obedient children was correct but her means of achieving this were often wrong. While I'm glad she's offering an apology, much of what she writes repeats the reasons parenting was difficult for her and asking for compassion.

She doesn't understand I've spent a lifetime in compassion and forgiveness, but what I need is space for my body and soul to heal. I don't need to turn my heart toward her when it's a big day for me. Reading her message, my compassion for her is there, as always. But there's also anger that she's intruding on my retreat. And grief—knowing she will never be able to offer listening, love, warmth, curiosity, connection, kindness, affection, or any of the other good things I need. She's too caught up in her hurts and wounds to see others.

I realize I won't be able to offer all those good things to the next generations if I stay tied up in her stories. It's time for me to let go of my hurts and wounds if I'm to live in joy and freedom.

As I facilitate the first spiritual retreat with Awaken, I am on my own Camino journey. It's as hard as anything I've done, and I'm in a vale of tears off and on through the retreat. My wonderful co-facilitator, Valeyne, a dear soul friend to me, is terribly sick with Covid for nearly the whole retreat. Instead of leaning on her for support, I'm bringing her soup and medication between sessions, while training a new faculty member. Another participant is coughing up a lung and hoping it's not Covid, while also supporting Val. The seven others must trust in The Great Love to hold us all because I'm at the end of my capacities. They see me at my most vulnerable, but we create wonderful things together anyway.

Something about my suffering keeps me human and engaged. I lean hard into my body's resources and even harder into the "Lake of Love" that we imagine as a community. Somehow, over the two weeks, I feel myself waking up to the true home inside of myself. Basia, our host, is a source of comfort and steadiness.

As I give up my attachments to my American family, I'm also giving up my attachments to the United States, feeling more European by the minute. Strangely, the grief is giving way to a new home inside of me, and a new grounding in these orange stones.

CHAPTER 11

WELCOMING WEALTH

*"Most of all, untie your soul. Give it room to breathe.
Let it play, unashamed."*

me

My parents met at a missions' conference and started dating when they shared a ride in my dad's car back to their university. My mom had been sent to university to find a smart husband, since she would "never make anything of herself," according to my grandmother.

When my mom was a little girl, her dad abandoned the family and was living with another woman for several years. Even after he returned, his mental illness kept him from contributing fully. He had multiple depressions and suicide attempts, due in part to the financial pressures of providing for a family of eight on his accountant's salary. Her mom, left caring alone for six children with an eighth-grade education, would get jewelry-making kits and other crafts, and the kids had to sell them door to door. My mom remembers being terrified and humiliated by those sales calls.

Stories differ, but one goes that on the day he died by driving his car into a bridge abutment while living with my mom's family again, his wife shook him from his sleep, shouting that he had to get to work and make money, and that he was "worth more dead than alive," referring to his life insurance policy.

When I was growing up, my mom was intensely angry with my dad for not becoming a missionary. She'd point in his face and say, "You tricked me! You said we were moving overseas, yet here we are in America with a regular job raising kids like everyone else."

In my mother's family, there was never any pressure to become a doctor or lawyer, or any job that provides a consistent income. Of the six siblings, four ended up living as missionaries in all corners of the globe. The value of serving God over getting rich ran deep, and poverty and struggle were meant to be part of it, along with the creativity of frugality. My mom's favorite cookbook was *More with Less*, written by the Mennonite Central Committee to help Christians consume less of the world's food resources. It included recipes based on lentils, whole grains, fruits and nuts.

Stymied in her attempts to be a good missionary and please her mother, my parents stood in front of our church to take a vow of poverty when I was 5, pledging to give away ninety percent of their income and live on the bare minimum.

My mom worked at the Christian school we kids attended, but refused to accept her salary, until the school told her that she must because of employment laws. She agreed, but insisted on paying our full tuition instead of the discounted rate she could enjoy as faculty, so she still didn't bring any money home. Every month my parents sat at the dining room table, paying the monthly bills under a "praying hands" image, while my mom held her head in her hands, "What if we lose the house?"

Her refusal to accept income had consequences for me.

I often felt hungry, either unable to eat the flavorless meals or making sure my younger sisters had enough to eat. I lived in constant fear we'd lose our home if my parents couldn't pay the mortgage, a fear my dad assured me was unfounded. I took on babysitting jobs and other work to do my share, and saved every penny.

I recognize that the money fears are not all mine, or even my parents'. They feel far more ancient and rooted in religiously-based decisions. My great, great-grandparents on my mom's side moved all the way to the United States in the early twentieth century from Kangaroo Island, South Australia, to help build the City of Zion in Illinois, which was founded ten years earlier by an evangelical minister as a utopian religious community. It was meant to be a theocratic city-state where the principles of his Christian Catholic Apostolic Church would guide all aspects of life. The city was free from corruption, gambling, alcohol, smoking, movie theaters, and medical doctors. The church owned the land on which the community was built, and it was planned to be self-sufficient, with its own businesses, schools, and governance, based on strict fundamentalist Christian morals.

If stories are to be believed, my ancestors gave all their wealth to the church to help replace the roof. But that money was used for other purposes, and they left the church in anger. However, they kept their respect for Christian missionaries, and their top value was to give money to missions if they couldn't do the best thing and become a missionary. While other families moved to the States to make it rich, my family was more about the kingdom of God.

My mom did all she could to serve the poor. She had one food budget for our family, which was meant to provide for the simplest, generic foods that could be purchased in bulk. Another budget was to provide food for "the poor farm," as it was called in our town, the kind of institution common before government welfare programs. We kids weren't invited to join her, and we wondered if those who live in the almshouse might be dangerous or insane. My mom's dad spent many Christmases in "insane asylums" as they were known, and she has a soft spot in her heart, especially at Christmas, for anyone who has mental health struggles. If any of my friends from the poorer part of town came selling wrapping paper, knives, or cookies, she would always buy them.

One part of me is intensely proud of my parents and family for doing so much for others and having such big, compassionate hearts. Another is furious about going without the food, clothes, vacations, and treats other families with less earning power can afford. It's one thing for parents to give away their money, another for the kids to be caught up in the sacrifices. The kids have no choice.

My belief becomes, "Don't even bother asking for what you want. It will be given to someone else."

When I'm 11, my mom sits me and my brother at the dining room table for a family contract. She writes in cursive on lined notebook paper:

Christi—July 31, 1983

Don't be obnoxious—try to be a joy to be with.

Be willing to be taught—don't be proud.

Put yourself in the other person's place.

If Michael and Christi behave hatefully, Christi will be punished by not being allowed to read leisurely for one month.

Second offense results in another family conference to establish a worse punishment.

It's signed, *"Dad. Mom. Chri$ti."*

I appear to be obeying and agreeing to the family contract and my punishment. My defiance is known only to myself, with the dollar sign instead of an "s" in my name. I will save enough money to leave this place and not come back.

Thirty years later, I'm sitting at a different table looking over thirteen pages of transcript from a coaching session. The only problem is I can't find any coaching on the pages. There's advice-giving, pseudo-therapy, and a lot of talk. There's nearly none of the presence, listening, powerful questions, and pure curiosity that are the finely-honed skills of a professional coach.

Simon has asked me to offer him free mentor coaching so he can check that off his list and get his professional coaching credential, so he can legitimately be named Director of Coaching Education and CEO at our jointly-developed training program.

I had happily agreed, giving away another couple of dozen hours without pay. I had already spent months writing the course curriculum and meeting with him to design the workbook and accreditation materials. But now I'm in a quandary, my heart sinking as I realize I've hitched my reputation to someone who doesn't know that he doesn't know how to coach, nor does he care.

Suddenly, it's plain as day. I've been coaching many years

longer than he has, and already hold a senior credential, yet I'm giving myself away. He's the CEO and I'm in the support role. He's going to make the money, and the contract allows him to go teach my materials with his best friend while I'm out in the cold. Why? Because I have no balls?

He says, "If I have to spend the rest of my days teaching people how to listen, just shoot me now," thus shooting down what I hold most dear. "I say, go big or go home! I want to train leaders, but this ICF coaching stuff is the quickest way to make money."

Quietly, I let this information sink in. I decide to go with my least-favorite, most frightening approach. Telling the truth, even if it kills me.

"Simon, I'm sorry, but I don't see any coaching on these pages. If you want your professional credential and if we're going to work together, I'm afraid you'll have to hire a real mentor coach, pay for it, and show you can pass the exam. I'm not willing to rubber-stamp this."

On the drive home from his house, I realize this is not the first time I've given away so much of my time and knowledge to others. It's the third. Three different schools. Three times I've built curriculum, shaped ideas, created real value, only to hand it over and watch someone else own it and stand in the spotlight.

I come home spitting mad. I let loose, my words sharp and hot, as I fume to Ben about what I've just seen. He listens, steady as usual, then says one sentence that lands: "When are you going to finally be your own CEO?"

He's been asking me about this for years. And I've always had excuses. I'm not a businessperson. I don't know how to be an entrepreneur. Being a CEO is exhausting. And scary. I don't have the money to hire support, and I can't figure it all out myself.

Today, though, the question lands like a spark on dry grass. It ignites something I'd been circling for years. I don't have to keep giving away my time, my intellectual property, my earned expertise for someone else's dream. I can build my own. I can be the one hiring people to support my vision. It's also more than that. What I have to teach goes deep. It's about pure alignment from the core of being, up through purpose and identity, values and beliefs, to break forth in powerful behavior. But to truly teach it, I must live it.

I hire a business-building coach. A deceptively sweet woman named Ellany Lea, whom I've known through Brené Brown's Daring Greatly and Rising Strong community of certified practitioners. On day one, Ellany invites me to an assessment of my inner archetypes, which I find fascinating, as a lover of Jungian depths. I eagerly answer all the questions and await my results.

Strangely enough, the inner "Prostitute" is top of the list. I'm shocked! Of all people to be a prostitute, I would be voted least likely as a faithful wife of nearly thirty years who barely engages in the mildest flirtations. I know this can't be correct.

But Ellany ever so gently invites awareness. She explains that the prostitute archetype doesn't have anything to do with literal sex work. A prostitute is someone willing to offer what's of greatest value to her for little reward.

Boom.

I recognize myself instantly. According to Jung, the prostitute symbolizes the part of the human psyche willing to sell integrity, values, or authenticity for survival, security, or approval.

It's the part that's willing to compromise. It asks, "What do I have to trade that will make sure I stay safe and loved?" It's the part of me that betrays me repeatedly, silencing my voice, letting me go along with things that don't seem quite right. All for the sake of belonging.

Thankfully, the angry voice of the prostitute can be leveraged to learn what I will not sell. Ellany helps me clarify my non-negotiables.

I want time freedom.

I want joy.

I want a legacy of communities of grace.

I want enough money for my family to live well.

I want to teach people how to listen and love one another.

It is a new way of living. I'm going to stop giving away my soul. And no one is going to die.

I tentatively ask Ben the most terrifying question, "Sweetie, would you still love me if I made a lot of money and was very successful?"

I'm quite sure he's not going to be pleased. He'll think I'm plunging into one of my big projects that will take me away from him. He'll be pissed off. He'll say, "Of course not! Who do you think you are to outshine everyone? Are you a narcissist? Why do you always need more? Why is money and fun so important to you? What will people think?"

Instead, my kind and generous husband says, "That would be awesome! How can I support you? This has been wanting to happen for a long time."

I can feel the reckoning coming. If he's going to love me even if I'm successful, then where are my excuses? I take a deep breath and decide. Here we go.

I wake on a chilly November morning in France in 2019, with the same paralyzing fear I've come to recognize in this entrepreneurial journey. My chest is constricted, my fingers curled, a knot in my stomach. It feels like I'm going to die if I can't figure out how to make enough money.

I've only had my Italian citizenship for less than a year, and I've got to learn how to be a business owner, which nothing in my life has prepared me for. As usual, when I panic about finances, my mind frantically moves toward getting a job and quitting this whole thing. Throwing in the entrepreneurial towel. The desperate need for financial security overwhelms me.

Something must be done about these intense money fears, and I'm determined to be free. I just don't know how—it seems bigger than me—and I'm not even sure it's possible. Money fears have plagued me my whole life. I decide to jump on an airplane (my solution to most problems) and go to a "Money Mindset" retreat for coaches, all the way across the world in Portland, Oregon.

I stand in a circle with a dozen other women entrepreneurs. Each of us is asked to shout out our "number," using facts and intuition as a guide. Our "number" is the amount of money we want to earn in the following year. The facts include our monthly bills like rent, food, clothing, taxes, etc. Our intuition adds information about what feels right.

I'm caught in turmoil, with no idea what my number is. I have waves of emotions as the other women shout theirs. One says, "Thirty thousand!" and I almost choke. Who can survive on so little? I dislike her instantly. Another shouts, "Two hundred and forty thousand!" What a ludicrous amount. Who needs to live like a princess while others starve? I shout, "Eighty thousand dollars," neither using facts nor intuition as a guide. It's just a number that won't get me crucified by all the people who have strong judgments about money. Ahem.

Next, we engage in an activity based on Gay Hendricks' book *The Big Leap*, which I've read on the airplane. Hendricks says that people stop themselves from operating out of their zone of genius and true potential because they have one of four hidden barriers he calls their Upper Limit Problem.

The first is "feeling fundamentally flawed"—you feel defective and unworthy, so you don't even know if it's possible to be successful and fulfilled. In me, it also shows up as the thought,

"I'm just not good with money." With that thought, I don't do the diligent work of keeping track of my money. I'm not even sure how much I make, and I'm surprised at tax time. The unconscious mantra of this fear is: "I cannot expand to my full creative genius because something is fundamentally wrong with me."

The second hidden barrier is about "disloyalty and abandonment." People caught in this refuse to expand and embrace success for fear of leaving friends and family behind. We ask ourselves, "Which of my family's unspoken rules will I need to break to get to where I want to go?" I recognize this thought pattern as well, and the punishment I would feel I deserved if I had plenty of income, as if I had lost my internal compass and values and abandoned my family. The unconscious mantra of this fear is: "I cannot expand to my full success because it would cause me to end up all alone, be disloyal to my roots, and leave behind people from my past."

Third is believing that "more success brings a bigger burden." I remember my dad never negotiating for a raise, but being annoyed when fresh, young employees earned more than him just because they negotiated. He consoled himself by saying that people who earn more just have bigger headaches at tax time and trying to figure out how to manage all that money. I find anything to do with numbers is a pain in the butt. The unconscious mantra of this fear is: "I can't expand to my highest potential because I'd be an even bigger burden than I am now."

And the fourth is "the crime of outshining" others. In this category, I recognize a strong belief that I can't be spiritual and make money. Making money makes it so much harder to enter the kingdom of heaven. It's related to the sin of pride, and thinking too much about myself. Success might even feel dangerous. I recognize this one immediately. To me, wealth and success seem like punishable offenses. I recognize myself living this out when I give more for less, when I discount my prices, when I give more time than I have. The unconscious mantra of this fear is: "I must not expand to my full success, because if I did, I would outshine _____ and make him or her look or feel bad."

Just being aware of these thoughts already brings relief, especially knowing that so many other people have similar thoughts. As a group, we decide that if thoughts of unworthiness, disloyalty, burdening, or outshining pop up, we'll wake up and realize that "this is just a thought". When we notice ourselves behaving out of those beliefs, we'll treat ourselves with compassion, accepting and loving ourselves into a new way of possibility.

I wonder if money can be an enactment of my spirituality. What if money is a neutral energy simply amplifying who I already am? There are kind and generous people in the world who are doing kind and generous things with their money. I'm kind and generous, too. I do good things with my money.

I've broken so many other family rules already. I've allowed myself more pleasure than I'm meant to. I've allowed myself to speak up when I'm meant to be quiet. What if I break their rules about money, too? I'll still belong to the people who matter to me most. At first, the mantra Hendricks recommends, "I expand in abundance, success, and love every day, as I inspire those around me to do the same," feels so, so wrong. But slowly, I let myself believe that expanding in abundance is good. Expanding in love is good. I'm not so sure about success, but when I think of inspiring others, I finally realize that these are all good things for me, too.

I think back to my all-time favorite book about money, Lynne Twist's *The Soul of Money*. For Twist, sufficiency is a beautiful practice rooted in gratitude. Net worth is not self-worth. Money, far from being evil, becomes a sacred tool when it's aligned with my values. If my purpose is to create communities of grace, where people can be loved and accepted just as they are, money is part of becoming spiritually aligned.

In my childhood home, jobs were meant to be places of drudgery where we earned money to give it away to charitable causes. Now, learning that money is a conduit of my values, I wonder if my work itself, and the money that flows through me, can be the spiritual path.

I imagine the flow of money like a giant garden hose full of water from a limitless source. Enough water will bring life to the land. Whatever quantity is wanting to come through me and my hose must have a clear passageway. If I reach back and put a kink in the hose before the water gets to me, I've blocked the goodness that's meant to flow. In the same way, if I allow the water to come my way, but then refuse to let it flow beyond me, I've blocked the flow lower in the pipeline. Either way, the soil is not nourished.

However, when I charge the true value of my service, goodness flows into both the person choosing the coaching, and into my life. I know coaching is in complete alignment with my values, and that the person making their purchase will receive immense goodness from our relationship, as will I. And I want to be able to sustainably continue this good work. So, I price my services in a way that honors the value to the client and allows me to continue offering my best.

In the same way, when I spend money in alignment with my values, I'm directing goodness toward things that matter to me— my kids' education, nutritious food, a beautiful home, experiences that draw us together as a family, and generosity to others.

Receiving money for sustainability in my coaching work is similar to a baker receiving money for their bread. If I want the boulangeries across France to continue to produce delicious breads each morning, I want to contribute for the flour, the hands that knead the dough, and the shop where neighbors congregate to make purchases.

Our money mindset retreat ends with a final, provocative activity. Twelve women sit in a circle, each holding a crisp $100 bill we've brought with us for the game. The bills are identical, but the dreams behind them couldn't be more different as each business is unique. The air hums with possibility.

One by one, we share our dreams and what step we're ready to take. After each story, the other women quietly decide where to place their bill. Some tuck it into the dreamer's hand, others slide it across the table, folded once, an act both practical and sacred.

As the money circulates, trust, belief, and courage circulate too. By the end, no one knows who gave to whom, or whose original bill we're holding. What matters is that each woman has been seen, supported, and reminded that abundance grows in motion. The circle isn't about the money. It's about permission to want, to ask, to receive, to give.

We find that, as long as the bills circulate, each of us can reach our dreams. We've got $1,200 between us, and with that small amount, we can offer one another support and encouragement to succeed. As that person moves toward their goal, they also need to support the other businesses. Money is neither created nor destroyed; it just keeps on serving us as it moves. We can all sense its spiritual power, and see the death knell that's obvious if one person hordes it or refuses to receive it.

Seeing the sheer abundance that soars from a limited amount of money in the hands of loving, dedicated women with big dreams, I realize my dreams are good. They are worth pouring my heart into. And our family's bills will get paid. We have always been completely loved and cared for. We will not lose the house.

CHAPTER 12

ABUTTING RADICAL EQUALITY

*"This morn let it be sworn
That we are one human kin."*
Amanda Gorman

I'm standing on tired legs, at the end of a long week on the factory floor. I'm counting down the minutes, and even the seconds until I can drive home, now that I finally have my license. The air rings with the thrash metal of Metallica, as it's Dan's day to choose the music. On my day, I choose a classical music station, mostly to annoy him but also to soothe my jangling nerves. My hands ache from gripping a heavy metal die, my ears ring from the steady thud of the wooden mallet striking the cutting block.

Our job is to roll out long bands of velvety filter paper used for biological testing. We need to make sure the die cuts cleanly through the paper with as little waste between circles as possible but not overlapping. There can be no tears or folds, and we stack the circles one-hundred-high in cardboard packages. It's the sheer boredom and repetition that dulls my mind.

Next to me, Dan keeps me sane. He works in rhythm—tattoos running up his forearms, sleeves rolled high, a grin that comes easy. He teaches me eighties slang while we work. His idea is to have a daily vocabulary exchange. We keep a notebook for our new words. He tells me I'm "wicked fly" when I wear something he thinks is cool. At the end of the day, he tells me he's heading to the "crib." When I say I need a "respite" instead of a smoke break, he doubles over laughing, shaking his head. "You're a f'in walking dictionary," he says. He watches his language around me.

On our smoke breaks, he and Sally give me life advice. Sally tells me she takes "wicked good care of my body," getting tested for AIDS religiously every six months, and recounting the details of the guys she slept with on her last vacation to Mykonos. Dan is careful to blow his cigarette smoke away from me, as he points out the deep symbolism in his tattoos. Nora, who works one table over, sits apart from the smoke, but loves to show us photos of her grandkids back in Colombia. She's been working on this same factory floor for nearly forty years. I'm barely surviving ten weeks.

I haven't been given much choice about jobs. Some of my friends work at McDonalds and Burger King, but my dad insists each of his four kids will work at least one summer on a factory floor, getting to know fellow Americans for whom this is their daily, monthly, yearly routine.

If he's to pay for our education at a private university, he wants us to know how valuable it is, and what life is like for the majority. Part of his job is to manage several factories. He regularly walks around talking to people, watching their movements for signs of repetitive stress, and deciding how to design the equipment so it's easier on their bodies. The company-wide joke is where he left his coffee cup that day. Probably on one of the machines that needs improvement.

Factory work is exhausting. Everything hurts. I jump into our family's minivan to drive myself forty minutes home and put in a Russ Taff cassette tape. It's not exactly allowed because it's rock music, but it's not exactly taboo either because it's Christian. Some of his songs like "Praise the Lord" are clearly in-bounds, but today I'm listening to "Ain't No Grave" and "Not Gonna Bow" because they're edgy, Pentecostal, and rebellious. It's a reminder that sometimes, instead of fitting in with this world, you can stand alone for Jesus. I want freedom and joy, and most of all, I want this long week to be over.

My left foot tapping, my right foot presses firmly on the gas, as I take the winding curves of a New England country road. I'm in a fifty mile per hour zone, and I am going sixty, as the road hits a residential zone where the speed limit drops suddenly to thirty. A cop car sits hiding in the trees, and the police lights flash as soon as I zoom by. The officer hands me a $90 speeding ticket, which has been doubled to $180 by the governor in an attempt to build more revenue for the state.

I look at the $180 ticket, and then at my $160 paycheck for my week's work. I could have stayed home all week and come out ahead! My eyes fog with tears for the rest of the drive home.

I don't have the heart to tell my mom, but I tell my dad the whole story. I ask, "How long would you feel upset about a speeding ticket?" He says, "About five minutes. Then I would be grateful that I can afford it. For some of those workers, that's their grocery money, their heating bill, their kids' lunches. They're not expecting to be paid more than minimum wage, ever. A setback like this would be devastating. For us, it's merely annoying. You know one day you'll get a high-paying job, and you know that your parents can support you financially."

On behalf of the factory workers in our state, he decides to help me write a protest letter to the governor, and later that year doubling speeding tickets is declared unconstitutional.

At rush hour, I'm inching my way past a donkey cart to my right, while a white and yellow *matatu* veers past me to the left, and I pull up to the parking lot of the university where my dad works. A security guard asks my name, and I give it along with whom I'm here to see. I'm there to pick up my dad to go to his favorite coffee shop, The Mug. Once in the lot, I circle slowly twice, looking for an empty spot in the convoluted L-shaped lot. When I ask security if he can help, he says, "There are no free spaces, you'll have to go park down at the Baptist Church lot and walk back up."

Just next to where he's standing is an open space, with a large orange cone blocking it. I turn to leave and head back out into traffic when a young man comes running out of the front entrance, shouting in a panic about who my dad is—holding the senior-most position in the building. The security guard begins apologizing profusely and moves the orange cone so I can park adjacent to the entrance and let my dad know I'm here.

When my dad first arrived in Kenya, he didn't have a title other than as a volunteer consultant to the not-yet-existent science department of a university. His first year in his new country, he tasked himself with interviewing the heads of the top one-hun-dred companies in Kenya to discover exactly which science classes, which skills, would be most useful to their companies and most likely to result in a quick hire upon graduation.

From these interviews, he built an enormous spreadsheet and began designing his twenty-year post-retirement project. First would be the school of nursing, then the computer science building, followed by a chemistry and biology lab. His beloved world of physics, which he's always dreamed of teaching (and had to settle on teaching us kids using mainly napkins at the dinner table) would have to come last.

Slowly but surely, navigating multiple political morasses along the way, the plan became a reality, with brick and mortar, and faculty and staff. As the effects of his work grew, so did his titles. He found the titles more of a nuisance—the bigger his office and the more tucked away in the corner behind a cascade of secretaries, the less he liked it. Much to his staff's chagrin, he insisted on an open-door policy, and would take time for students to chat. "How else am I supposed to stay in touch with the real needs, if I can't see the people who are going to use what we're building?"

It was the same at home. He liked to stand at the kitchen window, washing the dishes after dinner. Every morning, he cooked my mom two eggs and a slice of buttered toast and washed up her dishes after she finished. His neighbors, passing by the house, would reprimand him, "What message are you sending? A man of your stature washing dishes?" He would reply, "If people see me washing dishes, so much the better. The message is clear without words. We're all equal."

When my kids and I visited him, he loved putting a toddler high up on his shoulders and holding hands with a bigger kid, walking with them to the swimming pool across the street, just to see the faces of those who don't believe an older man should be seen caring for children.

Today, I tell him about the incident in the parking lot. I would have been happy to park a couple of blocks away and walk and find it amusing to be treated with such deference because of who my dad is. He's not amused, though, and decides to have a short chat with the security guard. He's kind and firm, telling the guard that in the future, the spot with the orange cone is reserved for real needs—emergencies or someone with a disability, and that I can walk.

Over a decade later, when I call the American embassy, the phone is answered by a young Kenyan man. I tell him my dad's name and that I need to set a time to pick up his death certificate. The man on the other end goes silent and I can hear him softly crying. "Are you okay?" I ask gently. He says, "Your dad was my dad, too. He was a dad to all of us. I hadn't heard he had passed. *Poleni sana.* I'm so sorry for your whole family."

We don't rush to get to business. Instead, I listen as he tells me that the project that made my dad the most beloved amongst students is that he re-engineered the university course registration process. When he arrived, students stood for days in the hot sun, negotiating for spots in the classes they needed for graduation. The course requests went through two weeks of negotiations in various committees, and students didn't always receive a place in the classes they requested. Seeing the long queues of frustrated students, my dad put on his engineering hat and got to work to find the roadblocks, just as he had done as the manager of a factory floor.

It took my dad nearly two years of heavy office politics to convince the school's senate that it would be a good thing that their work in the committees would no longer be needed once students could register online. His patience and respect eventually led to the whole process being reduced to a two-day smoothly operating online system, with no need to stand in line, and the highest possible ratio of students getting what they need.

Senior year, and I live in an off-campus house with beds for six people. One bedroom is a triple, with a bunk. The other is a double. And the last is a single room. I've never had a room to myself in my life, and at the beginning of the school year, when we all draw straws, I'm the winner.

I only stay for about two weeks. The three girls sharing the triple are at each other's throats. Samantha loves beauty and cleanliness and can't stand that Tina leaves her socks on the floor and a pile of dirty dishes in the bathroom sink. Tina, an actress and poet, can't stand the nitpicking. And Celia wants them both to stop fighting so she can get some sleep. She's got to wake early for her chemistry classes. When they've all had enough, they come to me to see if I'd be willing to switch rooms with Samantha, and I do.

If there are dishes in the sink, I can wash them. I've tripped on worse than socks before. And I like folding Celia's laundry for her because she has such a rigorous class schedule. We settle into our routines. I seem to be the only one who can get along perfectly with everyone in the house. I adapt myself to each one's needs and smooth things over. I don't need much. I'm just happy to be included.

The double room is occupied by two high-powered women with big career goals. In our final semester, one is off to foreign lands with a Fulbright scholarship, and the other has an internship at a conservative think-tank, The Heritage Foundation, in Washington, DC, which sounds equally prestigious. With their room vacant, we need two new housemates.

I've never met Kerri, who's just returning from the HNGR program in Nicaragua, and joins our house with her friend. She's just completed our school's version of the Peace Corps work, and I'm enthralled by her stories of service, all in Spanish. She captures my heart immediately, and I think she's the most beautiful person I've ever met. She has a gentle, warm laugh. Her gray eyes twinkle with delight.

She's dating a guy studying in Chicago, and they look like identical twins, with their brown, shoulder-length hair and huge, natural smiles. They started their relationship with years of friendship, which developed into a beautiful love story. They love to sing together while Fred plays the guitar. Their friendship is wonderfully soothing. Even though she has Fred, she takes plenty of time for me. We love to make pots of tea in the evening and talk for hours. I can barely believe my good fortune—that someone as wonderful as Kerri would want to be my friend. I do all I can to look out for her and make sure our friendship is solidified for life. She reminds me so much of my childhood friend, Jessica, as she is happy, vivacious and easy to love.

I worry we'll lose touch after graduation because we only have one semester together, and she's the kind of soulmate I've longed for since Jessica. But she invites me and Ben to her wedding after graduation, and we drive up on Ben's motorcycle. Her wedding feels a bit like love scenes from *Somewhere in Time*—the kind of ceremony you imagine in silver screen moments: a huge manor, sweeping lawns, water glinting nearby. Hundreds of people gathered under the large, white tent for a weekend of lavish festivities. Kerri and Fred take the extravagance in their stride, finding it part amusing, part annoying, and focus on their love for one another and not the stress their families create. Some famous Christian singers are invited, and I'm tongue-tied around all the glamour. Fred just laughs and dons an apron to help flip burgers.

During the ceremony, their simple love is on display. Fred brings out his guitar and surprises Kerri by singing in his own voice Keith Green's enchanting lyrics from *Love with Me*. None of us can hold back tears.

A year later, when my sister Kathryn joins me and Ben with only a few months' notice as a bride in a double wedding ceremony, she's freed up one of the bridesmaid dresses I've already sewn for her. With some trepidation, and very sheepishly for asking at the last minute, I call Kerri to see if she'd like to join the wedding party. She enthusiastically agrees. Her one fear is I'll ask her to shave her legs for the event, which she's willing to do, but she'd love to go in her natural state because she hasn't shaved since Nicaragua. I'm delighted she can come, and couldn't care less. I'll take her friendship in any state of hair-iness.

To my wonder, we stay in touch, writing regularly over the years. When Ben and I have been in Kenya for several years, she and Fred and their kids also move there, and we can rekindle the friendship we shared years earlier, like no time has passed. She lives on the far side of town, doing counseling work while Fred teaches at an American school. We commit to meeting regularly each month at a central location—an equidistant Java House restaurant.

She's so wise, so understanding. She's been a counselor for more than twenty years and has everything together, while I've remained a basket case, just now learning to coach. She gently teaches me that not every friendship moment is a coaching moment—while there are times to listen deeply, there are also times to let loose. When we meet, we text one another the night before to set expectations about if we want a pure friendship-style conversation, with lots of laughing, storytelling, and inter-rupting, or if one of us needs a more serious listen; she with decades of counseling skill, and there's me with my budding new coaching perspective.

I'm honored she'd take so much time for me and do my best to make it worth her while. I try not to overwhelm her with my traumas and dramas, but I feel like I take up more than my share of the talk time. Often, I pay for our coffees because she's giving me hundreds of dollars of free counseling. I feel enriched by our visits and humbled that she reaches out.

When our family moves to France years later, I miss her terribly. She tells me she's not one for texting, but she loves our in-person meetings. I still imagine she's forgotten me when I want to be texting her daily. I'm sure she has plenty of other friends who appreciate her loving wisdom, though she assures me not everyone sees her as kindly as I do.

When my dad dies and I return to Kenya for the funeral, Kerri is one of only two people who shows up for me. Not for my dad. Not for my mom. Just to be by my side. I never forget that kind of love. Funerals are not fun, and people who attend them are friends for life.

In late 2018, I'm finally prepared with all the paperwork in hand to apply for my Italian citizenship. I've got to drive from our home in France and live in Italy indefinitely while the documents are processed and I'm lonely. Kerri writes to ask if we might have a week-long vacation in Florence, and I can't contain my excitement. She purchases a ticket and makes most of the plans to see the statue of David, beating the crowds with an 8 a.m. appointment in the Accademia Gallery, mapping out visits for us at the Duomo, the Uffizi Gallery, and the Ponte Vecchio. My job is to relax and eat as much handmade ravioli as I can.

It's a magnificent week, and again I'm a mooch. I take up so much of her time with my woes and tell her stories of how hard it's been to deal with the more difficult religious leaders, particularly my missionary boss in France. I try to tell it all with a smile, not to burden anyone. But Kerri is serious. "Christi, you should not be telling these stories with a smile. You're being terribly mistreated, and it's not a joke! Don't you ever swear?" I admit I've never been able to let an F-bomb fall from my lips. The worst word I've said is "damn," and not too often.

Kerri's on a mission. I must learn to swear. Some situations call for real anger, and to tell the truth, with a lot of power. She squeezes my hand. "Honey, I know you love to forgive people. And I love you for that. But don't forgive too soon. There's a time for anger." She helps me to stand up on top of the bed and tell my stories again, this time shouting, *"Fuck you!* Yeah, fuck you for treating me like I'm less than you. Fuck you for your arrogance! Fuck you for stealing my joy."

I'm sobbing, shaking, and have snot dripping down my face. But I feel so much stronger and better. For the rest of the week, I walk lightly with so much of my chronic back, neck, hip, and knee pain miraculously released. I feel Kerri has healed me in a new way, and I'm incredibly grateful. The week is over too soon and ends with a call letting me know my citizenship has been approved. I can return home to France. Kerri is nearly as ecstatic as I am.

The next year, my mom orders me to accompany her to Kenya. She's afraid of traveling by herself since my dad died and needs me with her, to be on hand in case anything happens, but to stay out of her hair. She wants me there for the full two-month trip, but I tell her I can come for a week. I decide to bring Raven. It will be their first trip back to the land where they were born and grew up. Kerri gets us to a house on campus down the road from her and we only need to feed the owner's cat.

I try to stay out of Kerri's hair, too, recognizing she has lots of important clients to talk to and a busy family to care for. The week is frustrating. I'm annoyed to be at my mom's beck and call. I don't have a working sim card or my own vehicle, but I'm trying to figure things out as much as I can. Uber is on strike, so I spend hours standing in the rain, trying to get from one side of town to another. Sometimes I borrow Kerri's car and driver, but I try not to take advantage. I end each day exhausted. I'm keeping even more busy than usual in my attempts to keep my deep grief at bay on this first trip back to Kenya since the funeral.

As I pack my bags to leave the country, Kerri's pissed at me. I've been trying not to be a mooch, but I learn she wants something else—my company, my presence. She wants more time together. That is unbelievable. I think of myself as a burden, not a person people want to be friends with. By not knowing my worth, I starve her of what she wants. She says, "I guess I was expecting another Florence. I need more in a friendship."

I cry nearly the whole flight back to France. I've ruined a beautiful relationship, and it feels irreparable. I've been putting her on a pedestal and imagining myself so much less than she is.

What did she mean by "another Florence?" Did she enjoy our time as much as I did? Now I wonder if maybe she sees me as an equal? I review our friendship in a new light. Looking at the data, it seems possible she enjoys my company? Maybe she values our talks as much as I do? Maybe it's not even what I have to offer in terms of coaching or paying for things. Could it be that I'm good company? That I'm kind?

Unlike my painful friendship breakup with Jessica in sixth grade, Kerri is not rejecting me because I'm not cool or funny enough. She's upset because I'm not showing her that I value our friendship. I'm not sure which is worse.

I realize that if I'm ever going to restore this friendship, I've got to get some self-esteem. Self-esteem, in my mind, is just another word to make selfishness sound more palatable. I can't start with that, but I can start with a smidge of self-tolerance. And maybe even some self-compassion.

Through my training as a Daring Way facilitator with Brené Brown's organization, I'm following Kristin Neff's work, and her teachings on three parts of self-compassion: self-kindness, common humanity, and mindfulness. I'm already fairly decent at mindfulness at times. When I was pregnant with Leila in those difficult Paris days of panic attacks, I lay prone on the floor twice a day for forty-five minutes, following Jon Kabat-Zinn's voice through a body scan. I can still hear his voice in my ear, "The way you are feeling is the way you are feeling right now. Just accepting it..." I'm feeling like an extremely shitty friend, but

I can feel the way I'm feeling right now, just accepting it.

Self-kindness is harder for me. It involves being warm and supportive of myself, instead of being self-critical. I fill a notebook with all the kind words I wish others could speak to me. I write, "It's okay, sweetie. I see you. I love you. You're all right. You're a good person. You're kind. This is a moment of suffering—the kind many people feel at times." This is the opposite of self-judgment. I'm treating myself with the same warmth, care, and understanding I would offer a good friend like Kerri. Turning the same words toward myself. I can't quite feel it, but over time, I begin erasing past harsh voices with my soft and tender whispers to myself.

The third pillar of self-compassion is common humanity, meaning suffering and imperfections are a normal part of the shared human experience. I learn to toggle back and forth gently between pain and pleasure. I practice being present with my suffering without judgment. I'm careful not to stay in dark places too long, as I've always done. Instead, when the darkness is overwhelming, I balance it with another awareness. I ground myself through my feet, take a couple of deep breaths, do shoulder rolls, turn my spine, and remind myself I'm safe and okay in this moment. Pleasure and joy are also possible.

Over time, I let myself take a tiny peek at self-esteem, through the work of relational therapist Terry Real. Ben and I are miserably locked in love for one another that somehow seems wrapped in competition, in trying to get the other person to receive our love and failing. We can't figure out why marriage is so hard, and we sign up for a five-month marriage course with the Relational Life Institute.

Terry Real teaches that healthy self-esteem involves an inner sense of worth that is neither "one-up" grandiosity nor "one-down" shame. What Terry wants is for us to hold steady, neither better than nor less than the person next to us. Quoting the Irish proverb, "No matter how high or great the throne, what sits on it is the same as your own," he says, "My ass is the same as your ass."

True equality requires moving beyond these extremes to a place of balanced self-esteem, where a person can recognize their worth as inherent rather than earned through performance or superiority. He draws an image of a circle in the center between the extremes and invites us to sink into our heart space and feel ourselves alive and well there.

You can't be better or worse than someone else any more than you can add to your value or take from it. It's infinite and it is there purely because you're alive and breathing on this planet. There are no other possible qualifications, despite our patriarchal world's deeply entrenched attempts to train us otherwise.

In *Dead Man Walking*, Susan Sarandon and Sean Penn play Nun Helen Prejean and convicted murderer Matthew. In the last days before Matthew's execution, the nun serves as his spiritual guide. Before he dies, she realizes they are completely equal by virtue of being human.

I recognize grandiosity and shame in myself. I realize I almost systematically put myself in the "one-down" position, a painful feeling of being less than others. I'm not consciously trying to put myself down, I just see others as so beautiful, strong, wealthy. So successful. They are the glorious ones, while I'm just happy to tag along if they allow. They're on a pedestal, while I'm the admirer, hoping they'll notice me. I can see that Kerri is one of many, many friends I've aggrandized, though she's always shared her pains and struggles with me as an equal. With this realization, it will take some years to understand how we want our relationship to flourish.

Strangely, I also recognize grandiosity in myself. This is the "one-up" position I go to when I'm trying to prove I'm not a bad person. See? I'm strong, successful and beautiful, too.

I remember saying this out loud to our pastor when I was discovering grace in my twenties. It felt amazing that I might be talented and have strengths and skills like everyone else. But the pastor asked me if I might be struggling with the sin of pride, dashing my new-found willingness to think well of myself. I do feel a distorted superiority over others at times, which can feel briefly good. It arises particularly around my smarts and expertise, but I know it's masking my insecurities.

Either way, whether stuck in grandiosity or shame, they feel different from the balanced, peaceful state right in the center of inherent self-worth. I start to feel it little by little, what it's like to come home to myself. It's strangely relaxing. Just being here, in my body, without comparisons or judgments. It reminds me of floating on the surface of a lake.

Patriarchy has taught women to minimize ourselves, silence our voices, and believe that wanting pleasure, recognition, or equality is "too much" or somehow improper. I've been thrashing around in the ugly soup of patriarchy since before I was born.

The healing path seems to mean letting myself feel worthy before receiving validation and words of affirmation. It means learning I'm just as valuable when I'm hanging out doing nothing on the couch as I am when I'm holding court in a group. It means holding my inner voice against legacies of shame, being willing to speak up and to listen. To be both powerful and connected. It means being a strong leader while having a tender heart.

As I imagine staying in that healthy center, it feels like the tight band around my chest loosens. The breath moves more easily, deeper. There's warmth spreading from the center. Not dramatic, just steady and calm, like the body remembering something from many generations ago. Something known by the trees. My shoulders drop. My ribs rise and fall gently, without effort. There's no need to hold anything up. I can let down the sky. Inside, there's space, quiet and alive. I am here. I belong.

No one above, no one below. Just breath moving through a body that knows its place.

Micah is once again refusing to take a teaspoon of thick, red syrup—medicine for a pretty scary ear infection that comes with a high fever. We've been up most of the night. Trying to avoid the harsh flavor, Micah wildly flings their arms, knocking the spoon out of my hand and the bottle to the floor, splattering the sticky stuff all over the wall, the floor, and my bedspread. Frustrated, I grab their shoulders and shake, shouting, "You've got to take this medicine. Now look at this mess!" They stare at me with big, blue eyes, shoulders tense, and their little body rigid.

I can't believe what I'm doing. I promised myself there would never be violence, yelling, or name-calling in our home, that my kids would always feel safe around me. And here I am, shaking a little kid and screaming.

My initial anger is gone, replaced by a raw, scraping shame. My first attempt at fixing this is pathetic. "Look, I'm sorry, okay? But you have to take this medicine. Now half the bottle is wasted, and it's really important to finish the dose." I am still angry. It's the worst kind of apology, the "sorry, but" that invalidates the entire sentiment and puts the blame back on the child. I tell Micah I've got to take a minute to gather myself.

I walk to the campus clinic, dejected. With tears in my eyes, I tell the nurse what I've done. She's sympathetic and sits with me. "I'm sorry," she says. "I know Micah is sensitive. I should have offered you the pink medicine, which has an easier flavor for some kids." She fills the prescription a second time with another option. I'm amazed at her fluid apology, and the way she takes responsibility and comes up with a solution. I realize I need to learn to do the same.

Back at home, I sit with a book on my lap about the languages of apology. I realize my "sorry" is empty because it only serves me, explaining and justifying myself. The book lists five languages, and I see three I desperately need right now, and that are excruciating to practice.

I walk to Micah's bedroom and knock gently. They're on the bed, paging through a picture book. I sit on the mattress.

"Micah." They glance at my face to see if I'm okay. I wait. "I need to apologize."

I take a breath, clutching the book's concepts like a script.

"First," my voice is steadier than I feel, "I am so sorry." This is the first language: expressing regret. "I feel awful about how I spoke to you. It was not okay. Seeing the look on your face when I yelled and shook you... it broke my heart. I am so sorry that I caused you that pain."

I move to the second key: accepting responsibility. "It wasn't your fault. It was mine. That medicine was too disgusting for you, and I took my stress out on you. There is no excuse. It was wrong."

Micah looks at me full in the face now. Little kids forgive so quickly, but I want to make sure they know I'm serious. I need the third key, the one that proves I mean it. Genuinely repenting, which the book says is about the desire to change.

"I am going to work on this," I say, leaning in. "I promise you, when I feel myself getting angry, I will walk away and breathe instead of lashing out. You do not deserve my anger, and I will do everything to make sure it doesn't happen again. I got you a different medicine that tastes better."

Micah doesn't wait a moment, flinging their little arms around my neck and covering my face in tiny kisses. "I love you, Mom." I'm so humbled, not feeling I deserve it. "I know," I say, my throat tight, "I love you, too."

My attempts to avoid criticism, rejection, and blame are

exhausting. Apologizing feels harrowing for years, especially the part about saying, "I was wrong." But then it feels clean and free afterward. It's not difficult for me to feel bad and to feel with the other person but admitting wrongdoing and making amends is hard. The only thing that makes it easier is remembering I'm loved and lovable, like Sister Pat taught me so patiently.

This won't be the last time I need to apologize to my kids, who all seem to be way better at it than I am. I hear them apologizing to each other regularly, offering hugs, and making things right with treats and exchanges, and I wonder how they learned it so young. They make it look natural, and I don't know if it will ever be easy for me. One of them teaches me regularly how important it is to them to say the words, "I was wrong." Ouch, but good.

In a last-ditch hope of staying with the missionary organization who we have been with in France, hope built on the friendships and closeness that are still dear to us worldwide, I go to their international conference. There, in the presence of our pastoral support representative joining from the United States, I'll meet with my boss who was chasing me for a language report a week after my dad's funeral. The pastoral support representative is a gentle soul and kind listener. She's to be by my side as I tell this man truthfully what our experience with him has been, how it felt to have him not acknowledge my dad's death, and how his policies are impacting our family.

I have a short list of requested changes. His wife asks to join us, too, and we three women wait to begin the conversation. His wife is docile and has had the task of raising their children while he "preaches the good news" to Muslims and does church planting in the South of France. Ben is back in France with our kids.

Our boss doesn't sit. He paces near our table, texting and talking on the phone. He eventually sits briefly, without looking at any of us, and I do my best to speak through his numerous distractions. He ends up exploding and walking off, the meeting ends almost before it begins. I'm sure the pastoral support representative will intervene. However, she gently and meekly reminds me that he is the boss. Like it or not, my main job is to submit.

I have one more way to hold on to hope. I'm close friends with someone who is married to someone high up in the organization, a woman who's flown in from Thailand to participate on the prayer team. We naturally sit together on the bus on an afternoon outing. She's interested in how our life has been since moving to France, and I choose my words carefully, truthfully, and respectfully. Her eyes well with tears, and she squeezes my hand. "Oh, sweetie, that's so hard. I'm so sorry." I let her know that the current toxic leadership is damaging nationwide, to our French colleagues who have confided in us as well.

However, her next words are chilling: "Christi, I wonder if maybe it's time for you and Ben to think about moving on?" She reminds me that this man is in charge, that submission is our role, and I do need to look out for myself. The kindest thing for me is to leave.

The other shoe finally drops. This organization, from top to bottom, will uphold misogyny. Especially the kind, gentle women.

Ben and I begin quietly looking for another organization. I still don't quite have our Italian citizenship, so staying in France depends on Ben's clergy visa. But I'm no longer willing to be the free missionary wife, or to comply with misogynistic systems.

So, when we move to the next mission organization, we're clear from the start. Since Ben is the only one getting a salary, the only person listed on Social Security for tax purposes, the monthly reports will only mention him. Our results are not going to mention me at all. I will be building a private business and will not need to tell them my movements. Normally, a mission's family is supposed to be a package deal. Even the kids are tacitly meant to be model Christians. But this time they are not getting a free wife. Instead, I get to be free.

They make a few quick phone calls because nobody's tried to not be the free wife before and there's no policy. After some deliberation, they decide to accept Ben on the team asking only that I let them know if I leave the country, for safety purposes.

This new organization offers a delirious amount of freedom. We're allowed to raise as much or as little financial support from churches in America as we like, and we can follow whatever we believe to be God's call. We don't need to follow a standard procedure of moving all over France. If we have one church in America that vouches for us and acts as our "sending church" and we have an invitation letter from an organization in France, they'll make sure we receive our charitable donations, after taking their ten percent fee.

Thankfully, we've remained close with our French colleagues. The French side of the organization, which is as uncomfortable with our previous boss' domineering style as we are, is happy to send Ben a letter of welcome. Ben will now be the actual missionary, which is simpler for everyone. His work will be to offer spiritual accompaniment to leaders across Africa, France, and other parts of the world. He's always been an incredible listener, has years of coaching and spiritual accompaniment training as well as an international perspective, and has people clamoring for his presence.

I'm free to build Awaken, my coaching business, as an LLC headquartered out of the United States, so we're finally aligned with our passions, and our kids get to relax. The years of anxiety during our tumultuous move have taken their toll, and our highly sensitive kids struggle with digestive and sensory issues for years after.

After three years with this new organization, their policies change. In June 2023, their "Statement of Faith" includes that sexual experience should be chastity for those outside a monogamous heterosexual marriage, and homosexual behavior is immoral.

So far, so good because Ben and I are heterosexual, married, and committed to an exemplary sex life. We're behaving in a remarkably biblical fashion.

However, it's also Pride Month. Ben and I both have numerous clients from a wide variety of sexual experiences. We have plenty of open debates in our house about sexuality and gender roles. In our house, we're big believers in everyone having their own opinions, which we can listen to without judgment, especially since none of us has fallen neatly into the traditional roles our culture has assigned. I make it my habit to support my gay, lesbian, trans, asexual, and other friends and family members beyond the binary, as openly as possible. One tiny token of allyship, which I hope is not just performative, is to make a Facebook post or two every year during Pride and I do the same this year.

My public post is enough to trigger a conversation with leadership and a letter of termination. Ben will be paid through November, and then we'll have left the world of Christian missions. Our pastoral care couple who gives us a call is in a tough spot. They have a lesbian family member, but they've chosen to keep it quiet so they can keep praying with the team every day at 11 a.m. Now it's their job to kick us out.

The relief for us is enormous. Even though the family's finances are now squarely on the shoulders of Awaken Coach Institute, which comes with its own worries, we finally have our Italian citizenship, and therefore no need for visas. And we can proclaim our universal love for humankind, of every religion, culture, and sexual identity, without worrying about who will judge us for being too inclusive.

At Awaken Coach Institute, we start every cohort with carefully designed introduction questions. The answers reveal our common humanity. I interview each participant personally, getting their take on our stance of radical acceptance—that we agree to offer non-judgment and kindness first to ourselves and then to everyone else in the community.

As anonymized examples, a Baha'i community leader from Syria and a Kenyan farmer will share classroom space with a trans policewoman from the UK, a senior VP of global oncology at a big pharma company, and a recently divorced hairdresser from Ohio. People will join our course having just received a cancer diagnosis, lost their dad, moved to another continent, and struggled with a teenager refusing to go to school.

In our email intros, I ask, "What is an experience you have of being 'other'—different from those around you? What are your best personal qualities in a time of crisis? Who lives with you? (Please feel free to include partners, pets, domestic animals, and plants—whoever makes you happy in your home)."

People find themselves connecting with who they are at heart, in the dailyness of life. As they share their highest hopes for this time we'll spend together, and their fears and anxieties about taking this course, they don't have any idea about anyone's title or anything our society would call external markers of success.

We're people first. There's no way any person can gain or lose even an iota of value. It's infinite. People are made of love and are intrinsically connected.

Whether you're the person working on a factory floor, or the guy who keeps leaving his cup of coffee on the factory floor as he dreams up different ways to design the machinery, we all have bodies. That's what connects us.

CHAPTER 13

TRACING SENSUALITY

"In the blazing energy of being alive we sit here with the singing crickets."
Brigid Lowry

Waking early to get ready for another day in sixth grade, I stretch my skinny arms over my head. That's strange! Where's my shirt? I kick off the blankets and drop my legs over the bedside.

Hilarious! I'm completely naked. I had stripped off my clothes again when I got hot in the night. My pajamas and underwear lie crumpled in a pile on the floor. Dressing quickly, I run into the hallway to tell my sister Kathryn, "I just woke up stark naked. Isn't that weird?"

My mom looks at me sharply from her bedroom door, "Honestly! I know exactly what you were thinking, young lady. You better watch it!" Her disgust sends a shiver through me. I must have been thinking something awful. But what?

By seventh grade, my body is changing. I have round, hard

lumps under my nipples and some swelling that makes it hard to sleep on my stomach. Lying on my side is awkward because my hip bones are jutting out in strange directions where they hadn't.

I wake up one morning and go to the bathroom to find blood on the toilet paper. Oh, bother. It's my period starting. Since I'm more than a year younger than all the other girls in my class, I've already heard them talking about pads, tampons, cramps, pain, and mess for at least a year, so I'm not surprised, just disappointed that my life is becoming significantly more complicated.

I search under the sink for my mom's supplies and find an enormous pad to stick in my underwear. I take two Tylenol and put an extra pad in my school bag. When I change the pad at home later that day, I wrap it in lots of toilet paper and shove it to the bottom of the waste basket.

After a few months, my class is going to have a field day of games at a wooded campground with a pavilion for barbecues, a man-made lake, and tennis and shuffleboard courts. It's owned by our church. There's an annual swimming race out to the diving board in the middle of the lake, and I'm consistently the first there. I win the prize every year, but when I visit the bathroom in the morning, I realize I can't swim because "Great Aunt Flow" has come to visit.

I panic. The humiliation will be too intense if I can't figure this out, so I brave the dreaded tampons. Some people think using a tampon means you're not a virgin anymore, but my mom buys them, so it must be okay. I open the box and read the instructions, carefully opening the paper wrapper and figuring out where to stick the gigantic super-sized tube, which says it's designed for heavy nighttime flow. I think I've got it right, but it's so painful! How can women stand to even walk with a huge cardboard tube blocking their movements?

I go to the dining room for some cereal, but the pain is too intense when I sit, so I stagger back to the bathroom and yank the thing out. Reading the directions again, I realize that the cardboard tube doesn't stay inside, just the cotton. I try again, and this time, the misery is bearable, though the tampon is way too large and dry for my tiny body. The discomfort is worth it, though, to miss out on the humiliation if I had to explain why I can't swim.

The school year ends and over the summer I get more adept at the most comfortable placement of the tampons, which is a lot further inside than I had thought, so I can enjoy the local pond with my sister as usual.

One day, my mom is waiting for us as we return from swimming. "Christi, can I talk with you privately?" she says. My mouth goes dry, and my heart races.

She doesn't look upset, though, so I follow her into the bathroom. "Sweetie, there are a lot of pads and tampons in the waste basket these days, and my supplies are dwindling. Have you started your period?" I nod, and she asks, "When did this happen? Do you need me to explain to you how to use pads?" I say, "I've had it for about six months. Mom, I'm fine. I figured it out."

She bursts into tears and envelopes me in a huge, shaky, sobbing hug, which I squirm out of. "You're a *woman* now! We should have a cake as a family and celebrate. I'm going to tell all the ladies at church. This is wonderful!" She looks me up and down in tearful, joyful wonder. "Why didn't you tell me?"

I just motion up and down her body with both hands and say with contempt, "Because this. And please, no cake. Just let me have my privacy." I squeeze past her large frame and her even larger disappointment.

Danny sits behind me in class each year. My last name falls just before his. In seventh grade, I'm far more aware of his proximity.

He moves around a lot, pushing aside the blond hair that falls into his blue eyes, dropping pieces of paper near my desk, sending spitwads into my hair. I try to be annoyed but can't stop smiling. At recess, we run races, tearing across the field in one-hundred-yard dashes the other kids have marked out for us. He's fast, but I pump my legs hard, close enough so either one of us could win that day's race. I'm the only tomboy who joins the guys for soccer, and there's plenty of bumping into one another.

On Saturday afternoons, my sister Kathryn and I ride our banana-seat bikes two miles to circulate the block where his house is located. We pedal slowly each time we pass it, glancing toward the yard, hoping he'll step out and notice. Never once does he see us, though. We follow through on our pretense of stopping by the nearby convenience store to buy a ten-cent box of Alexander the Grape candy and start for home. We have no idea what we'd say or do if he came outside.

One Thursday, he asks me to go with him to our class roller skating outing on Saturday. At first, my heart soars. He likes me! Almost immediately, though, it begins pounding with fear. If I say yes, we'll be holding hands publicly as we circle on our skates to slow music under the disco ball.

There is no way my mom won't know. She works at the school, and news travels fast. I mumble, nearly inaudibly, "I don't know," afraid of even asking my mom if I can say yes, and terrified of what might happen if she finds out I didn't ask permission. He shrugs. He never asks again, and I never give him a real answer. Things are awkward between us after.

I start having dreams about him. They're always dreams of bondage. I never choose to be with him, but we end up bound together on a slave ship, our bodies pressed together because of our evil owners. I have the kinds of thoughts my mother would never approve.

The year I'm 12, and I've gotten my period, my mom decides

we need to have "the talk." She tells me very little, other than stating with disgust, "Just remember that all guys, even the nicest ones, are only after one thing. And the last thing you need is to get pregnant." She reminds me that my Christian witness is important, which means not causing men to stumble, and certainly never letting their hands anywhere near the button of my pants. Legs are to be kept crossed. She tells me that guys like having their balls touched, but it's gross and hairy, so I won't like it. Better to keep my hands to myself.

She emphasizes the importance of cherishing my modesty above all else. Plunging necklines, by which she means V-necked t-shirts, will definitely attract the wrong kind of attention. Rather, a colorful scarf near the face will draw the eye in the appropriate direction. I'm not sure the other seventh graders are wearing colorful scarves, but I don't protest because I just want this conversation to be over. I don't get to choose my clothes, and the bargain one-dollar orange turtlenecks she selects in bulk for me from the sale bin at The Fair are unlikely to get me into the kind of trouble she fears, with or without scarves.

I'm 14 and in Belgium for the summer. I've received a scholarship through my dad's work to spend a summer abroad. I'm placed with a stern but fun Catholic family with four children and am given a private bedroom in the loft. The boys are not allowed upstairs.

The family plans a day at the pool, and when I dive in, I come up gasping with my right shoulder dislocated. Pain sears through me, and things gray out when I look at my shoulder to see a hollow where a bulge normally is, and a bulge where there's normally none. My bathing suit slips down to my waist, and I can't pull it up with one arm. Three boys haul me up the ladder, pushing at me from below, my suit still at my waist. I would do anything to cover myself, but no one else seems to find it unusual that my breasts are exposed.

At the hospital, the doctor grins as he slips a mask with an anesthetic over my face. "Bye-bye!" he says in English. The room fades. I wake with a sling and a pounding head, embarrassed to have caused such a fuss on our fun outing. When we return home my host dad, a professional acupuncturist, offers his services, promising I'll feel much better almost instantly. I shake my head. The needles seem dangerous, foreign, too close to something I've been told is wrong. So, I wear a sling most of the time for the following weeks.

The next weekend the kids plan a biking trip without the parents. We bike about ten kilometers to a house by a river in the countryside. It has a large shed by the water's edge. The family's adopted son chases me around with a plant in his hand. I don't know what it is, so I don't even try to run away, until it burns my arm. It's a stinging nettle, the tiny hairs under the leaves leaving my skin sharp and hot. He laughs, and the next time he chases me, I run behind the shed. He follows, away from the bikes and the fields where the others are lounging. He grabs me, and his tongue flickers into my mouth, wet and snaky. I freeze. It's my first kiss, nothing like the gentle connection I had imagined. Stunned, I don't push him away. I playact for the rest of the summer, pretending it's what I want.

In my sophomore year at college, I'm seated next to a guy in my Spanish class whose eyes make me turn to butter. They're a deep, liquid brown, surrounded by the thickest black lashes. He's bad at Spanish, with the worst gringo accent, so he laughs at himself with the rich, confident rumble of someone comfortable being bad at things. I can't think straight with him sitting right next to me.

He compliments me on my Spanish accent, which I think sounds French. I'm not getting the hang of these rolled rs, so we practice putting our mouths in different shapes to make the sounds, giving me a great opportunity to ogle the soft lips that move smoothly over his perfect white teeth. My thoughts are muddled when he runs a deeply tanned hand through his masses of dark curls. The way he leans back in his chair pulls me toward him.

After class, I'm acutely aware of our strides hitting the sidewalk in tandem. His clothes are expensive, casual in the way that only money can buy. He wears a purple and blue jacket branded with The North Face logo, perfect for skiing at the Vail resort. Underneath, a thick Eddie Bauer sweater exaggerates his bulk.

As we arrive at the cafeteria, heads turn. People assume we're together by the way we laugh and move in sync, and I imagine that, to others, we look like one of those beautiful power couples in the movies. He tells me about the mountains of Colorado and his plans to take over his father's business after graduation.

It's hard to focus on his words, as I'm undeniably aware of aliveness in every part of my body. I'm filled with a liquid fullness, and my breathing goes shallow. I watch his mouth move and imagine his lips on mine. Leaving the cafeteria, I see his GMC Jimmy parked, big and glossy. He asks if I'd like to go for a spin with him, which I do. Very much.

Soon, knowing my love for all things French, he asks if I'd like to use the second ticket he's purchased to see *Les Mis*. Those tickets cost more than I'd earn in a week at my job at the travel bureau. The evening arrives, and he holds out his arm to walk me to his car. I've borrowed a low-cut, velvet evening gown, with a necklace that sits in an eye-catching place on one of my very nice curves. I can see he's looking approvingly.

The attraction between us is undeniable. My skin hums as I take in the soaring scenes and the big emotions of the French Revolution. Afterwards, he folds me in his arms, and we share our first kiss. The rush of power that surges through my body is astounding. It's not my first kiss, but it's the first kiss that's ever done this to me.

Over the next months, I float through my classes. I take lots of pictures of him and of us with the Canon camera my dad bought me for photography class. I'm excited to show my friends back home. They're never going to believe that shy, nerdy Christi ended up with someone so hot. I anticipate their wonderment and jealousy.

It's so easy with him. We meet up to try new restaurants, to laugh, to drive around in his Jimmy with the music on. Dinners out lead to passionate kisses that take my breath away. Laughter spills freely. It's pure pleasure. Just the lightness of being young, alive, and wanted.

I don't tell my parents about him for over a year, sure my mom wouldn't be pleased with me dating someone so rich and good-looking. But when he talks to me about marriage, and the big house he wants to build me on a mountaintop, and the wonderful European vacations we'll get to plan when he's making a fortune, I know it's time to break the news to them.

I anxiously meet his parents first, who've come to visit for a long weekend break. His dad's an enormous, dark-skinned Greek man with a powerful presence. He's not a believer, and he insists his son must be gay when he finds out he's following the Christian school's rules and hasn't already taken me to bed. I receive that opinion with some discomfort.

His mom moves with effortless elegance, with understated gold jewelry and professionally colored and styled platinum blond hair. I do my best to dress my finest while they're here, and to sound cultured and knowledgeable. She clearly approves of her son's choice and envisions me playing tennis with her at the 4H club where she volunteers. She tells me her son is to be the new CEO of the family business in two years, and he'll be hiring his younger brother as director. We women will have plenty to do while they're at work, with our various philanthropic projects.

I break the news to my dad over the phone that I have a boyfriend who I love, and that we're serious. I'm not ready to tell my mom, so I ask him to pass the word along. My dad is a prankster, and he immediately puts his "suitor evaluation form" in the mail to my boyfriend's college mailbox. My dad likes to send this form to any guy who looks at me for more than two seconds, and it's scared off more than one person with its ridiculous questions about whether they eat the skin on their potatoes and are completely potty-trained.

When the "Greek god," as he's known, receives his form, he gets right to work, confidently responding with hilarious answers. He writes that his main qualification for being my suitor is how strongly attracted he is to my body. But also seriously letting them know how much he loves me and how much he'd love to offer me in life.

My parents come to visit in their turn, and after meeting him briefly, my mom tells me that lust is nothing upon which to base a marriage. She doesn't approve of this "Greek god's" values. He seems entirely too focused on physical pleasures, and she doesn't see his spiritual depth. He's so wealthy she is sure I'd feel out of place, and she couldn't recommend I move forward with it.

I break up with him rather coolly. Tears roll down his face, which shocks me, and he begs to know why. I've never seen a man cry. I have no answer, and I honestly can't take in the fact that he could care so much. In a letter I write later, explaining why, I tell him he can't really love me, and that he'll get over me quickly and be fine. I assure him I'm not worth thinking about for another second.

The summer after I break up with him, between my junior and senior years of college, is the last time I'll need to find a place to be away from my mom's home. At nineteen, I go to France to stay in the home of a young woman, Juliette, who once stayed in our place as an exchange student. Now she's returning the favor and offering me a room in her apartment by the Place de Clichy.

Settled there, I think back with horror on what I've done. With a heart full of guilt, I remember my love's tears and I write a long, impassioned letter to the Greek god telling him what a complete idiot I am, how foolish I am to have given up so much, and begging him to let me come back to him. I wait and hope.

One Friday evening, a few weeks later, I receive a postcard at Juliette's from the Greek god. He wishes me well and gently lets me know that a mutual friend of ours, who I know has been inter-ested in him, has visited him a couple of times over the summer and to not be surprised if I see them together when the school year starts in the fall. I'm devastated and can't stop crying. I know I asked him to move on quickly, but this is much too quick. Maybe I am as forgettable as I tried to convince him I am.

Unable to console myself, I lose myself for days going to parties and bars with Juliette's friends. Juliette's gone on vacation for a week but calls in to check on me. I dance a lot, make out with several random men about whom I know nothing, and sleep it off during the day, calling in sick on Monday at the take-out place. It is owned by Pierre, a heavy-set balding man in his late thirties.

At work, I tell my teammate about my terrible weekend and that I'm alone in the house. Pierre overhears and puts a comforting arm on my shoulder. That night, at 2 a.m., I hear a knock on the apartment door. I open it to find Pierre standing there sheepishly. He says that he ended up staying out too late and has to be at the restaurant by 5 a.m. Since my apartment is closer, would I mind giving him a place to sleep?

Confused, I offer him Juliette's bed in the next room, and I go back to sleep. Minutes later, I find him next to me with his hand rubbing vigorously between my thighs. I freeze, but my fear kicks in and I leap out of the bed and run to the kitchen, breathing hard. He follows me to the kitchen and says, "I'm so sorry. I really thought you loved me." Not wanting to make any sudden moves that might get me raped, I answer, "Yes, of course I do. I'm just not ready for this yet." I tenderly stroke his face, hoping my acting abilities are Oscar-level, and ask him to be on his way back to the office. At work that day, and for every day for my last weeks in France, I feign interest, saying it's only too bad that I'm so young.

When school begins again for my senior year, I see the Greek god together with his new girlfriend, and my heart is torn in two. I can still feel him but can't go near him. I walk into my house and lean on the inside of the front door, sinking to the floor, wracked by sobs. My girlfriend's mom is there to help her unpack. She sees my grief and rushes to comfort me. She sits by my side on the carpet for an eternity, hearing my sadness, gently offering hugs, and letting me know in everything she says and does that she feels with me how painful it is to lose your first love. I don't have the heart to tell her I brought the grief on myself.

Three years into marriage, which we entered as virgins, Ben and I are still figuring things out. It's important for Ben that I really enjoy myself in the bedroom, and so far, our lovemaking has been more about quantity than quality. It's a mix of fun and frustration, even though our attraction is real. I love being in his strong arms and tearing myself away from him to go to work is agony. I could snuggle with him all day, and we often spend hours kissing and touching each other in front of the fire.

But everything else about sex feels like a performance or an act. Almost like I'm not really in my body, just going through the motions of something forbidden. Something I've seen on TV, but not something I'm truly engaged with. It feels amusing, but I can't seem to stay present enough to feel much. I'm showing all the signs of having fun, but I'm not fully in the experience.

Plus, we're clueless. Our combined sex education as a couple consists of Ed Wheat's *Intended for Pleasure*, a Christian sex manual first published in the seventies. In evangelical circles, it's the most widely recommended resource by pastors for engaged couples. Written by a physician, it's medical, philosophical, and grounded in conservative, biblical language. It's meant to offer permission to have sex for pleasure, not only for procreative duty, but it's not pleasurable to read.

The only way I can think of to learn more is to take a trip to Barnes & Noble. Ben and I go, awkwardly picking up books in the way-too-public section about sexuality. We are more interested than we let on about the various drawings and descriptions. We go home with a stack of materials, including Lonnie Barbach's book *For Yourself* about women's pleasure. These pages demonstrate that women can and should enjoy sex as much as men. I don't quite believe it, because my man enjoys it a whole lot.

Next, we brave a discreet shop that sells sex toys and buy the world's least dramatic egg-shaped vibrator after walking with our heads down past a lot of anatomically exaggerated dildos. My new books tell me to try the showerhead in the bathtub. I do start to feel a lot more sensations, but nothing like what would cause the heaving bosoms and cries of passion in a Nora Roberts romance novel.

I'm stubborn, though. Determined. There must be more than what I've experienced, and I will not let my mom's disgust and caution keep me from what I'm sure can be a whole lot of fun.

One afternoon, alone with a novel on the bed, I touch myself, trying again. At first, I feel nothing, just the voice in my head saying this is wrong, indulgent. That pleasure is dangerous, selfish. That good girls don't want.

Then a flicker. A pulse I almost miss. I press on. And then it happens. My body releases in waves, quiet but real. Not over-whelming, but enough to know it's not dangerous. It's not bad. It's mine, and it ends with a feeling of peace and utter relaxation. The muscles throughout my body feel less tense than I can ever recall.

After that, I practice more often. I learn to signal to Ben without words what I want. He's generous, patient, gentle, and responsive. There are more than a few moments of frustration. Slowly, I let go with him, too. The story I grew up with—that sex was for men, that women endured it—loses its power. My pure determination to break the rules is paying off.

I realize I want it. And it's allowed. Pleasure isn't something to squeeze down. It's something to invite, to grow into, to let unfold. I tap into my powers of imagination, bringing in vibrant imagery that feeds my sensations. To climax, I must be selfish, focusing only on me, my body, this moment.

Over time, instead of cherishing my modesty, I cherish those times of complete aliveness when a wave can start from my core and travel down to my big toes, and all the way up through my face and arms. My body feels like a bright white lily of the field, grounded and glorious. Each experience leaves me peaceful and awake for days and becomes a fuel that makes me want to hum and sing with the joy of being alive.

CHAPTER 14

THE PATHWAY TO CHOSEN COMMUNITY AND RADICAL INCLUSION

"Be grateful for whoever comes, because each has been sent as a guide from beyond."

Rumi

My mom flies to visit my sister and me over spring break at college. I'm a senior, and Kathryn's a freshman. Ben and I have been dating for about a month, but my mom is itching to meet him. I have a sleepless night before her arrival. He can handle just about anyone, but my mom is a force of nature.

Ben stops by my house in the morning to say hello and see if my mom needs anything. She's about to walk across campus to Kathryn's dorm and is worried about getting lost, so he offers to walk with her. They set out across campus. Four hours later, they return, never having made it. He whispers to me, "She really grilled me on my theology, but I can read her well. I think things are okay."

After he leaves, she is glowing with approval, almost effervescent. They had gotten caught in conversation—topics of theology, faith, and a life in missions spilling back and forth between them. She is thoroughly impressed with his worldview and his heart of service. She extols his many virtues, and how thoughtful and steady he is.

Relieved and delighted, I ask if she thinks it will work out. She looks me straight in the eye and fiercely says, "You stay away from him! He's too nice for you. You'll walk all over him, and he doesn't stand a chance. You need someone who can give you a good beating when you need one."

Her words land hard. I swallow, but it doesn't go down. I feel small, my hands balled in a helpless fist, like I'm 2 years old again. I want to argue, to tell her she doesn't see me, but the words won't come. Instead, I sit in silence, crushed by her judgment.

Later that day, I decide to let her know how hurt I am by her words, thinking she'll soften. Instead, she assures me that, though the whole world is bound to tell me what a wonderful person I am, it's her job to be honest. If I'm getting a big head, she's the one person called on to cut me down to size. What I really need is for someone to tell me the truth about how spoiled a brat I am.

I make her lunch and long for Ben's return. It begins to snow heavily, in a late spring storm, and I see Ben calling me out to the field behind my house for a good snowball fight. I've been taking a self-defense class, so I try out some of my moves on him, trying to knock him into the snow. He's unmoved, crossing his arms and laughing at my feeble attempts. I keep charging at him until he pulls me down in the snow in one swift move, stuffs snow down my collar and drags me by my pant legs up the field.

We're shouting with laughter, and he pulls me up into his chest for a huge bear hug. My mom, washing the lunch dishes, is watching the whole thing from my kitchen window as he bests me, again and again, and I keep coming back for more.

When I come inside, she nods with a smile. This changes everything. Now she knows he can handle me.

In my quest for community, I create them for everyone except myself. I see the loneliness in the world, which reflects the loneliness in my heart, and I respond to others.

In 2018, spending weeks alone in a house in Italy, I wait for my Italian citizenship papers to be approved, not knowing if I'll be there for weeks or months. I'm in solitary confinement much of the day, other than the company of Jenny the dog.

Solitude is agonizing for me, an extreme extrovert. It always brings wonderful gifts, though. I spend hours under the hazelnut tree, writing in my journal, thinking, dreaming. I'm meant to wait until the police arrive to check that I live here. The hazelnut tree begins to speak to me, offering me downloads of brilliance.

I recall the years in Kenya after completing my two-year course in spiritual direction. Being the only non-Catholic means I don't have an immediate use for the training in a church diocese. Instead, I ask the leaders of a Kenyan retreat center if I can use their lovely grounds as a space for silent retreat days. They are delighted that the wider community will get to enjoy the space, so I send a simple invite to a few guests using Mailchimp. Each month, the list grows until more than sixty people are invited to the gatherings.

What's most interesting is that the retreat center is open and available every day. Anyone could come at any time and spend a day lounging in the grass. But the simple fact of an invitation draws people. I get emails asking, "When is your next silent retreat day?"

My invitations consist of saying, "Please arrive at 9 a.m. for our intention-setting gathering. Plan to remain in silence until at least 4 p.m." That's it. I never miss a month of these silent days of reflection for years, and at least six people attend each time. These days are so meaningful to people, and I can see how we're growing up together.

The first six people to sign up can have a short session with me in which we sit quietly together, asking Love what it will have them know for today. Others can simply come and rest, have a cup of tea if they like, draw, or journal. I offer a series of simple prayer prompts, like Bringing Emotions to God or Noticing the Five Senses. People often ask me in wonder how I can be so peaceful, which reminds me that keeping one's mouth shut is a great virtue.

One day in Italy, the hazelnut tree says to me, "What if you invite people to France for a week-long retreat, and you simply follow the same rhythm as your silent prayer days? What if you call this retreat 'The Beloved Community' and follow it with ten months of community-building based on Martin Luther King Junior's principles of the beloved community?"

I jot down ideas—what the retreat space will look like, how many bedrooms, the views, the type of people I want to invite, and how our days will be structured with a children's book each morning, followed by intention-setting and movement. Then many hours in silence with options for artwork, poetry, walking, and journaling. And closing each day with storytelling around the fire.

The retreat builds itself in one Saturday afternoon, including a year-long group coaching program, complete with journaling prompts about loving oneself, one's friends, and one's enemies.

The following morning, I attend a church service in Italian and begin scrolling through my phone during the sermon. A text arrives from a woman named Kate, whom I haven't spoken to or heard from in thirty years. She tells me she's living in the UK and has just bought a home in France. She wonders if I'd like to use it, free of charge, for a retreat. Tears roll down my cheeks with the shock of the serendipity, just as I'm called to the front to introduce myself as a guest for as long as I'll be in Italy.

I return to the house to start work on the website sales page for this gorgeous new idea. But before I can even post the page, I've already sold out the retreat. The retreat location has ensuite bedrooms for each of the four women who have already decided to sign up, and for me.

They arrive in France, each with their journey unfolding in dramatic ways. Our personalities are widely varied, and we meet with some trepidation wondering who we've just signed up to do our best to love for a year. Each of us offers gifts to the others: food, movement, artwork, poetry, touch, and heartfelt listening. Each of us returns home changed. We covenant together to speak the truth of our stories for a full year, meeting monthly in a group, and with individual coaching calls in between.

At the end of the first year, our hearts are full. We agree to continue meeting for a second year. Our calls continue to be life-giving for all of us. It's my honor to provide the container for the emergence of each person's becoming.

As the third year begins, the group of women ask me a pointed question. This year, rather than paying for a year of coaching, they'd like me to join them as a community member and take turns each month hosting the space.

First, rejection sensitivity kicks in. My initial response is to burst into tears, believing I'm not valuable, that my services aren't needed, that I can be replaced. It takes me weeks to hear what they actually asked. Far from rejecting me, they want me to share my stories as an equal, a human, a person. They want to know me.

That's a whole separate challenge. Having spent the first two years in the relative safety of the Wise One persona, now they're inviting me to share in the snotty noses, the anger, the messiness, and despair of being human. With a huge, scared inbreath, I agree.

My plan had been to create a network of Beloved Community groups, each kicking off with a retreat in France, followed by a year of group coaching around community-building. The idea was to combat loneliness at scale, in a world of increasing disconnection. But, after only the second group formed, Covid shut down the possibility of in-person gatherings. We were all grateful to be able to meet, and more in need of connection than ever.

The Beloved Community group becomes my most trusted, close-knit group of friends I've ever encountered. We're consistent, kind, and boundaried. We know how to listen without advising, how to own our stories without encroaching on others. How to speak our thoughts and emotions, even when it's difficult. Sometimes people need to take a break and come back. No one needs to believe something just because the others do. We have our unique interests and support one another in those.

Since our original meetup in 2019, we've gathered in one another's homes in Seattle, Doha, Bartenheim, and Denver. We've supported one another through the births of six babies, and the launch into adulthood of five grown children. No topic is off-limits, and we share the best and worst of parenting, marriage, work, and everything else. I can be inordinately proud of myself or caught in a shame storm. Either way, these women are here for it.

They teach me daily what real friendship means. I don't have to perform. There is nothing to prove. I know I'm loved no matter how poorly I'm behaving, and still seen for my strengths.

On March 11, 2020, I stand in the Tel Aviv airport, having just met with old and new friends in Israel-Palestine, who, with differing histories, are passionate about creating spaces of common humanity.

Staring at the panel of departing flights, I watch as airports shut down across the world, including my returning flight to France. In that moment, I receive a download, *"It's time. Awaken Coach Institute must be birthed as a place of community, connection, and courage."*

Until that point, I am deep into the heart work of professional depth coaching, both one-to-one and in groups. I have spent thousands of hours in conversation with women and men who want to tolerate, accept, and even love themselves, and be part of creating beauty in the world. It's been my soul work since my life and worldview were turned upside down by coaching in 2009.

In that airport, it becomes crystal clear that what the world needs is for a lot more of us to listen better, to see one another, to witness one another's stories. It's time for me to teach others how to be a person together. The world is about to become a far lonelier, more polarized place. We need to lean on one another in trusting, courageous relationships that bring a much larger effect than any of us can do alone.

On my flights home through Istanbul and Zurich, Awaken Coach Institute comes alive. Just three months later, our tiny team launches a brave pilot program with just ten early sign-ons. Our online coach training soon becomes a community. Our first cohort graduates that year, and Awaken Coach Institute continues to grow into a place where people learn not only how to coach, but how to live from courage and love.

My hope for Awaken remains simple: we're a brave, whole-hearted, global community for coaches who want to go deep.

We're there for people seeking a spiritual, meaningful path for themselves and others. We're training wonderful coaches who build deep connections across cultures through fully embodied listening. Together, we create a world that includes everybody, where everybody feels they belong—awake, alive, beloved, connected, and expansive.

The depth and level of what we offer our community is like no other coaching program, growing in love along with me.

I start walking alone through a thick mist by 8 a.m. The last of the four guests to leave the world's worst hostel in Spain, with its lumpy pillows and cramped metal bedframes, I enjoy complete solitude for more than two hours, barely able to see the Camino trail ahead. A wide variety of bird calls cut back and forth through the air. Occasionally a stone house peeks through the trees at me.

The more I walk, the more peaceful and full of love I feel. Memories of my Beloved Community sending me love letters for my birthday, and the heart connection with Ben from the day before continue to warm my soul. I feel comfortable in my skin, and at home in the world, an odd feeling for a global nomad, who hasn't known where home is in decades.

It's been a lonely quest over the years. I'm married to a man who was born in transit and who hasn't lived many years in his "passport countries." He's been a visitor, observer, stranger, from before he was born. Being between worlds feels like home to him, and he doesn't experience the lostness and loneliness that's my companion.

We've raised three children, born on three continents, who have no answer to the question, "Where are you from?" Of the five of us, I'm the only one who would say I'm American, though we all have the passport. I'm the only one who lived in the same house throughout my childhood and went to the same school from kindergarten through to twelfth grade.

I have felt the questions clawing at me so often in the middle of the night. Who will my people be? Who will be the witness to this one little life? Will anyone remember I've passed through this country or that one along the way? I've put a lot of pressure on Ben because he's my person. My one person. Everyone else will walk a kilometer or two, a day or two. He's the one I count on.

I recall a conversation a week earlier in Portugal. Simeon, a fellow pilgrim who can easily walk thirty-five to fifty kilometers a day and still have energy, slows his pace to mine and lets me pour out to him the near desperate urgency I often feel, wondering where home is and whether I will ever feel settled again. He asks, "Does any place along this Camino feel like home to you?"

I had thought the answer would be as shrouded in mist as I am right now, but the answer is strangely clear. I'm starting to feel at home everywhere. Each little village I pass could be home. I can imagine myself learning the market, the grocery store, the bank, the neighbors. I can create community out of thin air.

More than that, I can feel myself at home inside of my body. I am home.

Instead of a cramped heart space, I can feel vast mansions and lands inside. To feel at home inside my body is to finally set my luggage down. I am no longer a frantic, temporary guest, looking for the next apartment, but the owner of the estate, and the estate is thriving.

My interior world is a populated village. When I listen, in the mist, past the noise of the outside world, I hear it. Down the pathways of my nerves and along the routes of my veins, there are a hundred people talking and laughing, gathered around tables for copious meals. These are not the sharp, critical voices of self-doubt; this is the murmur of a community.

These are all the parts of me, the child who climbs hemlock trees and runs to the lake with a canoe over her head, the awkward teenager stumbling to fit in, the adult gaining power, and the wise, wonderful woman I will become. All are gathered. They are having warm conversations around a fire, sharing stories, holding space. No one is shunned. Every voice matters.

My breath moves through this village, a constant, steady breeze. My heartbeat is the rhythm of the village clock, ringing out *I am here, I am here, I am here.*

And this village is not confined. It sits in an impossibly vast landscape. I can walk through it, feeling the gentle rise and fall of my own hillsides, the solid, reliable ground of my being. There is grounded strength here. I can stand on a high ridge, a moment of pure clarity and truth, and look out. The vistas are endless.

I see the lands of my past, not as burned forests, but rich valleys I have already walked. Ahead, the territory expands as far as the eye can see, onto open, rolling land that invites me to explore. My skin is not confining, it is as fluid as a lake, defined yet touching the sky.

There is so much room. Room for a deep sadness to sit by a river and not flood the town. Room for a wild joy to run across the open plains without a fence to stop it. I am the landscape and the one walking it. To be at home in my body is to know I am not just a single, small thing.

As Walt Whitman says, "I contain multitudes." And I am, at last, a citizen of my own country.

We're on a family camping trip when I'm about to turn 12, and as my mom and I walk to the washrooms to clean dishes, we pass two women laughing and talking. My mom leans down like we're co-conspirators. "You see those women? I think they're *lesbians!*" I'm shocked, "Mom, why would you say something like that? You don't know them!" But she insists that you can always tell. Just by the way they're laughing a little too loudly together, and their hands keep brushing. Just look at the diving necklines on their shirts. She leans forward and says she bets they *slept together* last night in this very campground. I purse my lips. This is no way to talk.

By senior year in high school, I'm a fervent kid, praying constantly for my friends, and they for me. Two of my closest girlfriends, Erin and Courtney, have been kissing, and it's scary! We all know it's wrong, but it just seems out of control. They can't seem to stop, but it must stay a big secret.

My mom and their moms want me to spy on them and report back so they can "pray with discernment," and I'm terribly conflicted. More prayer warriors sound like a good idea, and I know I should trust the moms to help us, but it also seems like gossip. And what will the moms do, anyway? I opt to pretend I know nothing.

When Erin goes off to college to another state, it seems like things between them will end, and everyone will come back to the Lord. We continue talking, calling, and writing. In a letter from Erin, she is effusive, thanking me for yelling at her. Getting frustrated shows her that I care. She intends on praying more and knows with God's help she can get through it.

Later, she joyfully writes that things are amazing—all sorted out with her and Courtney. They can just be "two Christian friends who pray together, read the Bible together, and serve Him together, and the rest will fall into place."

However, the following Christmas, Erin comes to my house for a sleepover. We're in my grandmother's big brass double bed in the basement, staying up all night talking and laughing. Until the conversation takes a serious tone. "Christi," she says, "I have something important to tell you that you might not like." I sit up, ready to listen. "I'm a lesbian. This is who I am."

I'm honored that she's letting me know about the sin in her heart, and I squeeze her hand, committing to pray for her with even more zeal. But she says, "No, I don't think you get it. I'm not trying to repent of this. Now I know that this is just who I am. I plan to pursue a serious relationship with a woman. That's just who I'm attracted to and it's what I want for my life."

I hardly know what to say. One of our mutual friends has always taken the attitude, "Who cares who someone loves? It's none of my business." My judgmental mind thinks this is just letting them off the hook and not taking a stand for the truth. I love Erin, and I can tell she's not backing away from this. I feel helpless, and we fall more out of touch. Decades later, I'm finally able to apologize to Erin, who is joyfully, fully alive and married to a woman named Patty. They love travel, athleticism, and creating artwork together.

In college, Vanessa, who is energetic, vivacious, loud, and has a huge, infectious laugh becomes a dear friend. We block off time in the common room down the hall in our dorm to do aerobics. Blasting out *Electric Avenue* we do our best Jane Fonda moves in our aerobic leotards, cracking ourselves up. We're into wild amounts of hilarity, or deep discussions about philosophy and our deepest hurts and fears. Anything but small talk. It's a friendship for a lifetime—we know we'd do anything for each other.

Two decades later, Ben and I join a Christian mission organization for the first time—something we had sworn we would never do since Ben had grown up in missionary culture and knows the dark underbelly. From what I've seen, it's a strange culture I want no part of. However, when our kids are in upper elementary school, we realize they can't stay in the local Kenyan school system on the university campus. Our kids' lives are on a different, international trajectory. Getting an international education with a mix of Kenyan and international students is dramatically more expensive, way beyond our reach, but huge discounts are available for missionary families.

Our family has been living on a few hundred dollars per month, enough to live like any other Kenyan family of students, while Ben works on his PhD. Now, we're in Kenya far longer than anticipated as Ben's invited to support other doctoral candidates with their research and teach some classes. Our savings from the sale of our house in America are dwindling, especially after the 2008 stock market crash. To stay in Kenya, getting a missionary visa, little as we like the word "missionary" with its connotations of colonialism and evangelism, looks like our best option.

On our nearly four months long deputation tour for an organization that is the most maverick-style missions agency we can find, with few creeds to sign on to, and no policies, we're now in Georgia about to catch my electric-sliding college friend Vanessa for a quick coffee. I'm excited to see her after all these years, but she looks subdued. After we've talked a good half hour, she asks if she can talk with me out of earshot of my kids.

She lets me know she's a lesbian, and that coming out was a really painful experience in her conservative Christian family. In fact, she was so anxious that her hair went white overnight when she decided to tell her mom. Now, she's ready to tell me, too, and would love to introduce me to her partner. But she wants to be respectful and doesn't want to say anything in front of my kids in case I've been teaching them that her identity is morally wrong.

My eyes fill with tears as I imagine how difficult it must be to have to check with every friendship and carefully decide who's allowed to know. Who's safe and who's unsafe? Who's going to judge you, pray for you, or try to convince you you're wrong. And who you can just be yourself with. What a painful way to live, calling on daily extraordinary measures of courage. I wonder out loud how hard that must be, and she admits she's lost many friends and family relationships but being herself is life or death. I wonder if I'd have the courage to be fully myself and say what I think of things that are important to me.

I hug her hard and tell her that of course I'd love for her and her partner to meet my family. And that I have no intention of training my kids to judge anyone. We're overjoyed we get to rekindle this friendship from our college days, and sad that it's not a given. It takes a long time to build old friendships, and she's one of those amazing people I'd never want to lose.

In my heart, I vow to be far more vocal and outspoken about my love for all people of every gender and sexual expression, and to learn and grow all I can, so never again will anyone have to wonder if being themself is okay around me.

EMERGING PEACE

"Stand still. The forest knows where you are.
You must let it find you."
David Wagoner

We're at a conference in Florida with our missions agency. They've told us at the beginning of the week that education specialists will be watching our kids carefully for any anomalies, and that if they notice anything, we'll be called into a meeting at the end of the week. Ben and I have no worries. Our kids are smart, funny, kind, and doing well in school. At the end of the week, though, we're on the list of families that need to be talked to.

Our plan is to wind down our time in Kenya and move the family back to France. We've decided we can't stay in Kenya until Micah turns eighteen and then send them back to the States alone, so if I can have my Italian citizenship recognized, we'll move to France and keep the family all in one location. Micah always needed a little more gentleness and handling with care, and we can't throw them to the wolves just because they can't get a visa at 18.

But the assessors inform us we'll need to stay in the States for neurological testing for Micah, and that we can't move to France until we've figured out what's wrong with our eldest. They tell us, "We don't have enough information to make a diagnosis, but there's something different about Micah. When the other kids are jumping around, excited to go to Disney, Micah is slumped over, leaning on their arm. Micah stays apart from the other kids during lunch. They're obviously very bright, but there's just something off, and we can't put our finger on it."

We're stunned. Micah's always been quirky and funny and needs a lot more help getting food they can eat but has been very well-loved by everyone and is doing fine. They are creative and have written a book, chock-full of metaphor and intrigue. They get straight As at school. The whole family loves them and appreciates their peaceful way of connecting us.

The US is not home for us. Our lives and friendships, school, work, are all in Kenya. We don't have a place to live in the States and it's expensive. A family of five can hardly camp out on someone's couch indefinitely while we look for doctors to assess Micah. School is about to start.

After some negotiation, the missions agency agrees we can return home, if we send them a complete medical analysis by December.

Once home in Kenya, our friend Shelley, who lives in London, says she's happy to talk with Micah on the phone. She's a special needs specialist, and her son who's the same age as Micah was diagnosed with autism at just five months old. She thinks that even over Skype, she'll be able to at least send us in the right direction.

Shelley interviews each family member about our experiences. My heart cracks open listening to Leila explain how she supports Micah with friendships at school, heading over to the middle school to make sure Micah's included in a group before rushing back to the elementary school. How she looks after them at home. How did I have no idea?

Micah talks about how hard it is to be so often in the nurse's office, judged by the sports teacher for supposedly faking fainting and fatigue when running track in gym class, their difficulties finding nourishing food that's also swallowable, and often feeling sad and lonely.

Shelley recommends we speak with an autism specialist, and other tests are done in our home. An occupational therapist asks Micah to walk down the hallway, eyes open, eyes closed, feet in a straight line, standing on one foot, no hands out. Planking. Drawing a star on a piece of paper. The tests are not like I would have expected as they seem to be more related to balance, core strength, and physical coordination than anything to do with my idea of autism, which would have been an image of a young boy rocking in a corner.

I do all the tests with Micah, and have the same troubles with balance, walking in a straight line, and moving my fingers, but I'm not the one being tested. The way Micah tests all seems normal to me and a lot like their mom.

Next, we speak with an autism therapist on the other side of Nairobi, a British woman who is gentle, warm, smart, and witty. She tells us she herself is autistic, that she's single in her mid-thirties, and that if there's any diagnosis, we can still expect a wonderful life for our child.

She talks with Micah for hours, making copious notes about how Micah uses language, how they interact, the interest they show in others, or lack thereof. I feel my stomach clenching as the normal, everyday things we love about Micah, and that make them uniquely Micah, are charted out into a set of neurological differences that have names.

The world stops turning for a while.

My mind comes back to the room to meet my body. I find myself waking up to hear the therapist ask, "Do you wish to have a diagnosis? It's not an easy decision. If I give a diagnosis, it can change the way you and others think about Micah. For some people, having a label is unhelpful, so I can write the report so that family and teachers know best how to support the physical, emotional, and language needs without saying autism spectrum disorder (ASD). On the other hand, if you think you'll want support services paid for by the state one day, it can be very helpful to have a qualified therapist write the words down and could save you years of being on a waiting list to be seen by a specialist in someplace like the UK."

We opt for the non-diagnosis report. There are no services we're aware of in Kenya, our family is used to the way we are, and we don't see how the government will offer anything more than we can do at home.

The therapist talks with me separately. She wonders, "Have you ever felt relieved that Micah, at sixteen, hasn't shown interest in boys? I know for some parents it can be nice that they don't have to worry about their kids getting into trouble. But for others, it can be worrying if their child doesn't date, and they are concerned about whether they'll find love and a family one day. I'm here to tell you that I'm autistic, my sexuality is different from the typical, and I'm doing just fine. I have a lot of love in my life. It just might look different for your child."

She gently adds, "It's rare to see an autistic child who's so well-loved. Your family has created this beautiful cocoon so that Micah feels like a welcome part of the family. So often, I see parents who are incredibly angry, and who call their autistic child lazy, selfish, stubborn, or strong-willed because they can't comprehend that the child has physical and emotional needs. Then the child is angry with the parents and shuts down or lashes out. It can be a vicious cycle. In your family, please just continue doing what you're doing. If you do start looking at your child differently, I hope it will only bring more compassion, kindness, and understanding. The opposite can be devastating."

I tell the therapist that Micah's kind treatment is mainly thanks to my husband. I find myself frustrated at times and feel the urge to parent like my mother—to discipline and force Micah to step up and do as much housework as other kids their age, to force them to eat what's on their plate, to make them hike the mountain and go camping with the rest of the family. Ben seems to have limitless patience and understanding and can eat the same meals many times in a row if it helps Micah eat.

What's known as the "Ritvo Autism Asperger Diagnostic Scale" is easy to take at home, so I take the assessment to see what a normal score is like as I fully assume I'm "normal." The categories are language, social relatedness, sensory motor, and circumscribed interests. I fail to see the relation between the categories, but, apparently, they are combined to add up to a threshold for suspected ASD. The name is infuriating. Who's to say that Micah has a disorder?

I check my scores, and I'm well over the threshold. My social relatedness score is on the line between autistic and allistic (non-autistic) neurology. That brings a slight smile, as I recognize my strange, lifelong ability to bridge conversations between the misfits and the normals. But the others, especially language and sensory motor skills, soar high over the line into autism.

The aftermath takes weeks. We're all reeling. My autistic cousins are overjoyed to welcome us to the fold and info-dump about "the trifecta," telling me about ADHD, OCD, bi-polar disorder, borderline personality disorder, depression, anxiety, autonomic function differences, rejection sensitivity, PDA, EDS, hypermobility, POTS, mast cell activation syndrome... The list is overwhelming. I can't understand most of the terms and I have to stop looking at it.

What it means to me first, which is not necessarily what's most helpful to Micah, is an overpowering compassion for my mom. I can see all the traits of my mom immediately. Her rashes and allergies to grass, dust, and other unavoidable substances. The way she's always bumping into things, losing her balance, and dropping stuff. Her love for simple, bland, overcooked food. Her high anxiety. Her wild mood swings. Her lack of friends. Her disgust for sexuality. Her fixation on how clean and shiny the faucet in the bathroom sink is. The way she corrects strangers' grammar.

I think back to my mom's childhood—her dad's multiple suicide attempts, her mom's brutality and anger toward her, the ostracism she felt in her home as the unloved child. What if she were one of those many autistic girls who were completely misunderstood and mistreated in their homes and society? I remember she told me her mother used to chase her around the house with a two-by-four screaming, "You'll never make anything of yourself! You're so lazy."

What a scary, lonely life. I imagine what would have become of our little Micah if we had screamed at them, called them names, and hit them? I can't imagine. I refuse to imagine. Our precious, sensitive child would have broken. They wouldn't even be the same person.

Finally, I allow myself the indulgence of feeling a taste of that same compassion for myself. I begin to weep. Though I haven't owned the word "autism" for myself, I see the awkward, shy little girl in me who was called selfish, lazy, and evil. I want to reach down and scoop her up. I see her tender heart.

I see the viciousness in me, the hatred, the tight-fisted defiance. And I wonder if it's too late to love myself into being fully who I am. Made of love, like us all. I want, more than anything, to offer a huge basket of love for my mom, myself, my child and for all those who feel "other."

I glimpse that if I'm ever going to bring my huge heart of love into the world, it's going to start with loving me, which seems like a plenty big enough task.

I'm standing in my kitchen, if standing is the word for it. I'm leaning heavily on one elbow on the kitchen counter, the other hand on my lower back. I'm talking excitedly to Alice, an Awaken contractor who's come for a few days of intensive meetings in 2024 about our marketing strategy. This is just the way I stand. I've been in chronic pain since I can remember, having normal conversations and activities while blocking out pain that's generally around a three out of ten.

Today, I've tweaked something, which isn't unusual, so I'm hobbling more heavily than usual on my toes and struggling to straighten up. The pain is more like a seven, but still not all that unusual for my day-to-day. Alice stops me and says, "We're calling my friend Victoria Salomon. You can't be in pain like this all the time and just keep going." She picks up her phone and video calls Victoria on WhatsApp. "Hey, Victoria! Look at how Christi's walking," and she asks me to walk across my living room and back. Victoria covers her mouth with her hand. "Well, the good news is that you're hurting yourself! Which means you can stop."

I take the phone from Alice's hand to learn more. "Oh, Christi, your body is showing the classic presentation for pre-verbal physical abuse. I wonder if that rings true for you?" I'm reeling. How can she know that from watching me walk for twelve seconds? It's not something I talk about or tell people. Most of the time, I keep it a secret from myself. So, I ask her.

She tells me that abused kids are the only ones who walk like that. My feet are not connecting with the ground, and I'm curled forward in a protective stance, like I'm wearing a curved shell on my back. This strikes me as another data point that helps me believe my experiences. She explains to me that when little kids learn to dissociate from their bodies, it can take time and tenderness to be able to feel again that they're actually a person inside. A very valuable person worth cherishing, and who might not need so much protection as an adult.

I imagine a pangolin, which is the only mammal wholly covered in scales that they use to protect themselves from predators in the wild. Under threat, a pangolin will immediately curl into a tight ball and use its sharp-scaled tail to defend itself. I don't have any predators in my life, but it still feels like my back is covered in protective knives and my stomach is contracted. Along with the pangolin image, I can see a vision of my mom, her back dramatically curved in the same stance, but even more exaggerated. I know she's been badly hurt, too.

Victoria asks if I'd like a little pain relief, even today, with just a small training. Of course, I think that will be great. She invites me to feel my left foot on the ground. I can't feel much. In fact, I have almost no sensation in my feet, which is normal for me. When, several years earlier, I was fitted for shoe inserts by a podiatrist, she had me stand on pressure sensors to map the forces on my feet. When she saw my foot map, she looked at me with compassion, "With this kind of map, you must feel anxious and sad so much of the time. I'm sorry." My eyes welled, but I told myself not to have a pity party.

I had lost a lot of nerve function in my left leg after a botched ACL surgery in my knee, but foot sensation is almost nonexistent on both sides. I've bought one of those pads with electrodes on them that you can stand on. They deliver small electrical impulses to the feet to help manage pain. The dial goes up to twenty, and I can't even begin to feel the pulses until they reach twelve, and I'm very happy with the gentle electric stimulation when it's already at twenty. When Ben tries to use it, he yelps and pulls his feet away at a three.

She asks me to feel into three spots on my feet, the foot tripod. They are the heel, specifically the part that has a bone inside it toward the outside of the foot, the base of the big toe, and the base of the little toe, which she calls the first and fifth metatarsals. This natural tripod helps distribute weight evenly, maintain balance, and provides a stable base for movement. But I'm standing on the inside of my heel, where there's no bone for stability, and on the side of the first metatarsal.

It takes a while, but I can eventually feel all three spots on my left foot and that I've got a somewhat more stable landing pad. We do the same with the right foot. Then, she has me bend the right knee gently forward and notice what happens with my right hip. After making this incremental movement several times, I can stand nearly straight, and the pain in my lower back has lessened by half.

She asks me to turn slightly to the left and right. "Oh, my dear! We've got work to do! You have *no* idea where your boundaries are. You turn far too much from the knees and hips, well beyond a safe range of motion, while the strength in the arches of your feet, and the alignment of your ankles, are not helping you."

She's got another call, but I'm glad to have been helped this much for today, and I sign up for her seven-week program. It's the most grueling exercise program I've ever done—not because I appear to be doing anything at all, but because I have my bones lined up correctly and am using a different set of muscles.

When I find both foot tripods, even with my toes up on a pair of socks so I can feel my metatarsals and my feet on the floor at once, my whole body shakes. Even twenty minutes standing properly on my feet feels like I've been working out with one-hundred-pound weights. It's exhausting! I keep practicing a little every day until standing on my whole foot feels natural.

Each week, we focus on the bones deep inside my body that are solid and can be counted on. She invites me literally to stand on my own two feet. I learn to feel the talus bone in my ankle, from the inside. This brings a flood of tears. I can't explain, but I can feel a deep release.

Victoria is always respectful, recognizing me as a fellow professional in the world of creating more courage, freedom, and love. While I start with thoughts, emotions, and identity beliefs, she's beginning with the bones. We're partners with The Great Love in this work.

We move up the body slowly. Knees, femur, pelvis, spine, rib cage, shoulders, neck, and jaw, in that order. Each week, more tears are released. My pelvis doesn't budge much, and we do all kinds of positions from lying on my back, on my side, against a wall, to see if it will loosen into place from its stuck anterior tilt. It's stubborn, and I have minimal movement.

Each week, the shaking in my muscles is overwhelming. We meet over Zoom in a group of less than a dozen people. If you were to watch us without the sound, you'd think we were just a bunch of people standing still, doing nothing. Who would know how hard we're working?

The most dramatic emotional releases happen in my rib cage. I've never noticed my rib cage much before, and I hadn't realized how far it's been sinking into my abdomen and constricting my breathing. The rib cage really is like a cage. I can feel its structure protecting the heart and lungs. I want to give those vital organs as much space as I can, so they can fill my body with oxygenated blood and energy for life.

When my rib cage snaps upward and backward into its proper place, I cry off and on for two days. Suddenly, I'm standing tall, shoulders naturally back, my breasts at first feeling like I'm showing them off to the world, but over time like they're a normal, healthy part of my body. When I walk, I can feel my weight moving firmly down my back body into my heels. With the rib cage opening my heart, my pelvis loses its spiky, protective tail and softens downwards.

I can also vaguely feel how the muscles connect to the base of the rib cage. The psoas muscle connects to the lumbar vertebrae at the lowest rib. It travels deep inside the body, twisting over the front of the pelvic bone, turning back again to end at the top of the femur. With this muscle now needing to change its position with the new position of my ribs, I have dramatically more strength in my thighs, which have changed their shape significantly, lengthening in the front, and stronger in the back.

Now, instead of tiring after standing for just a few minutes, I can count on the bones in my pelvis, femur, knees, calves, and ankles to provide stability. When I go to my Thursday movement class and Sunday improv in the park, instead of requesting a chair so I can sit while the others stand, I take my place in the circle and move freely.

The shoulders also slowly release with great emotion. The clavicle that was broken during a diaper change when I was two, and the multiple shoulder dislocations have me tentative about moving my shoulders, especially overhead or to the back. It takes everything in me to trust I can count on the muscles in my back and chest, because of my newly aligned rib cage and spine. Instead of curving forward so my hands rest naturally on the fronts of my thighs, my arms swing smoothly and land naturally to my sides, which makes my back and shoulder blades feel powerful. I can feel my heart and lungs being protected, even while I open my heart space to receive so much more love from the world, both in front of me and behind me.

I'm not sure I'll survive the jaw work. As the tension dissolves in this area with proper bone placement, I feel a warmth and tingling in my face running down my body. A surge of strong emotions leave me wondering whether to laugh or cry. It's such freedom to stop the clenching, and letting loose here allows my pelvis to gain more flow and movement, too. After the initial rush, I feel a profound relaxation and lightness through the jaw radiating to the rest of the body. I'm tired and sleep for twelve hours, waking to wonder, "Is this how people normally live? Free and relaxed without pain?"

The rushes of love come unexpectedly. By the end of the seven weeks, I can barely remember what it was like to stand in any other way than both feet pointing straight ahead, my chest lifted with my back strong and belly soft. It feels like confidence without arrogance. Like decisiveness without authoritarianism. Like love without fear. I can breathe.

I've always known that health is multi-layered. Good sleep, quality nutrition, and emotional support from a community are all part of a coach's daily regimen of self-care that's the foundation to serve others. Now, I'm learning how essential the bones are for complete alignment and purpose. For many months, I keep going back to the free Monday evening check-ins to remind myself that my bones are on my side. They're trustworthy.

As I look over my two columns that I have spent a quiet afternoon working on, it's not black and white. It's not even about deciding which column is correct; it's about remembering that two things can be true at once. There's not so much certainty. There is some truth in what religion and a strict upbringing taught me. Like everything else, each perspective is true, partially.

My upbringing taught me...	A coaching mindset taught me...
I must be certain. There are truths and falsehood. Black and white. Heaven and hell. Reward and punishment.	I can find beauty and power in paradox, multiple perspectives, curiosity about experiences, and living with an open heart.
Sex is private and gross. Don't talk about it. And don't enjoy it.	My body is lovely and made for pleasure. I enjoy the power of sensuality and sexuality.
Anger is wrong. Forgive quickly and seek peace.	Anger is my body's signal that a boundary has been violated. Anger will stay alive as a friendly messenger until what's valuable is restored.
Suffering is holy. What I want and what God wants are opposites. If I want it, it's wrong.	Deepening my desires, clarifying my wants, and moving toward what I love is a way to know I'm living in the heart of my spiritual purpose. My desires are my North Star.
Emotions are deceitful. Instead, go to the Word of God for truth.	Emotions are wise powerhouses. Naming, listening, and befriending them, and getting to know the parts they represent can guide me to a deeper knowing.
To whom much is given, much is required.	I'm thrilled to be part of it all. We all get to be lilies of the field.

My upbringing taught me...	A coaching mindset taught me...
Women in the workplace are too much. Women in leadership are too much. Women are too much. I am too much. Confidence is a sign of pride.	Confidence, radiance, power, and joy are glorious in a woman. It's appropriate for me to take leadership when I have good things to offer.
Wealth is evil. Rich people are evil. Money should be given to the poor.	Money is like an irrigation system—it brings life and growth wherever it's sent. When money is freely earned, spent, and invested in alignment with loving values, it serves the world.
I know.	I wonder.
Don't trust yourself. You're sinful and evil.	I can build habits of trustworthiness—apologizing when I hurt someone, keeping confidences, behaving in line with my values. It's okay to disappoint authorities, but it's not okay to disappoint myself.
Don't trust yourself. Intuition is woo-woo.	Trusting myself and my body's insights comes with a deep peace and reassurance.
I will never find home on earth—my true home is in heaven.	I am home inside my body. I'm home because I'm human. I'm home in this moment. I'm home because there's enough love for me.
Evil doers should be punished.	Everyone is doing their best. Compassion and radical acceptance are powerful healers.

The churches and schools I've attended, the systems I've participated in, and my parents have done tremendous good in the world, despite enormous trauma and abuse in those systems. I wish my mom, especially, every blessing and health. I hope she knows deeply that she's loved and lovable, just because she's alive and human.

In fact, there are no bad or evil people in my family. There are dysfunctional systems, though. Dysfunction happens when caring people have been wounded and are trying to fix and save others instead of receiving love and taking responsibility for themselves. I include myself in that dynamic. It is through my experience of Love, which led to Leadership, Responsibility for my wrongs and finally to Resurrection. The more I feel loved, the more powerful I am, and the more I can take ownership of my mistakes and live out of joy.

If only I can get my mom to see how lovable she is, to forgive herself, to feel how precious she is, then she will be able to love me. So, I give, give, give, give. And get disappointed.

I realize that no one can make someone else feel loved. So, then what?

Try it with someone else. If only I could make my husband see how lovable he is, to see that he's precious even if he's not a good Christian missionary like his mom hopes, that he's fun and interesting, then he will be able to love me. So, I compliment, praise, hype up the fun, listen for hours. And wonder why he's annoyed.

I realize no one can make someone else feel loved. So, then what?

Try with the kids. Tell them they're amazing. Tell them they're wonderful. Tell them they're beautiful. Until their eyes roll.

I realize no one can make someone else feel loved. So, then what?

Then luuuuuuuuuv on everyone at Awaken. Make them feel like they're part of a warm, mom hug. Love them like they've never been loved before. And some will still move on. Hmm...

I suppose I could notice the love that's already there. Live in that for a while. It does seem like adult life is in large part about outgrowing childhood wounds, and learning to receive love, just the way every newborn is wired. The more I can't stand people criticizing me and cutting me down, the more I invite that behavior. But when I let go of those hurts, others are far more likely to treat me with appreciation.

Sometimes human love gets blocked, but even then, we are all being held by The Great Love. None of us would be alive today if we hadn't been loved into life by hundreds of others, even if sometimes poorly. We're created by the measure and multitude of our collective experiences.

Learning to sit in complexity means staying with discomfort. I don't need to solve the polarities. Complexity means I can see the humanity in myself and others with curiosity, and without needing to win, fix, or categorize. That's what freedom looks like. Not knowing the answers but knowing I can hold more and more each day.

I've seen a meme going around in which a grandparent is screaming at a parent. Then the parent screams at the child. Everything is dark, thunderous, and rainy overhead. Then the child grows up, "breaks the generational trauma" and is all sweetness and light with their child, and the sun shines brightly as the next generation grows up beautifully! Amazing!

In my experience, everything goes way more slowly than that. My parents could parent a little bit better than their parents. We probably did a bit better than ours, starting off with so many more resources. I still did some crappy things. My kids are going to need therapy. It's an achingly slow multi-generational turning of the tide.

I'm growing up in my fifties in ways I couldn't in my twenties. Our adult kids watching us grow up is a part of it. The key is to keep coming back to Love. The more I experience being loved, the easier it is to keep on owning what I did, keep on learning, keep on growing. Kids forgive so easily—they're wired to love their parents with all their hearts, whether or not we deserve it. And parenting is like a twelve-step program, learning to tell the truth, calling on a higher power, apologizing and making amends.

It's the story of the nations we participate in as well. We grow up and heal as communities and countries when we tell the whole truth. We own up to enslaving millions of people, killing off those who protested our empires, and creating hierarchies where some are valued more than others. And yet, we bring ourselves compassion. Owning our whole stories, while knowing we're loved, is the key to healing.

The great paradox is that the more we stick with the 'I'm good' narrative that's tied with our idealized identity, the more we continue to hurt others. It's like our idealized identity—that extra two percent shine—forces us to become evil. However, when we own our faults, and love ourselves through them, we find ourselves to be whole.

With this in mind, I go to the beach with my coach, Karin, imagining a long timeline, stretching generations into the past. In this vision, I walk all the way back to my grandmother. "What do you need?" I ask. "What would have made it possible for you to love my mom?"

My grandmother tells me her wounds, her loneliness, what it was like to raise six children alone with a husband who left for another woman. She tells me she needs support. To be seen. To have someone take on the tremendous load of work. I imagine the universe bending to offer her all these things and more. She's receiving strength, courage, humor, support, and relaxation.

I walk further along the timeline to my mother's birth and see her surrounded by her parents and older siblings. They're delighted to exclaim, "It's a girl!" There, my mom is cherished and held. She's filled with goodness and joy, content to explore and go on many marvelous adventures with a secure home base.

I walk the timeline, seeing my mom grow more and more loving and warm, until she's 25, welcoming me home as a newborn. I see her and my dad safe and secure, able to weather the storms because of their strong connection. I see their joy, "It's a girl!" they cry, at my birth. They don't give me a feminized male name or wish that I had been born Christian instead of Christi Anne.

They look on in wonder, as if watching a tiny acorn growing inevitably into a strong oak. They call me Emma, which means feminine wholeness. It's me. I can see the world clearly, with eyes delighted by the sheer beauty of being alive. My innate creativity guides me onward from their loving arms into a world where I can be part of the love all around.

I realize it's never too late to have a happy childhood. I can offer my little self all the gifts she needed, too. I can grow myself up with as much connection, courage, creativity, and compassion as a girl could ever need to be part of co-creating with the divine in this beautiful, difficult world we inhabit.

What I can see and feel in me, I can observe in you, too.

You're already loved. Now.

WALK YOUR OWN LABYRINTH

To walk a labyrinth is a quiet, yet revolutionary act. It's so different from standing on the edges, watching someone else walk it. Once you step in, and you're putting one foot in front of the other, you're entering into rhythm. You're surrendering to a timeless moving meditation.

It is the refusal to take the shortest distance between two points, opting instead for the sacred detour. The path is not a puzzle to be solved, but a surrender to be lived. It reminds you that in the divine geometry of your life, you are never lost, even as the path turns on itself.

I created The Awaken Way as an open invitation as you find yourself longing to walk your own labyrinth journey. I'm offering you this four-lesson experience because I want you to access the epic pattern: the inward journey, the center, and the return.

In this course, I've poured some of the deepest gems I've learned from my own journey as a coach, as a leader, and as a mother. We're all walking each other home, and my hope is that these four lessons will be a trustworthy companion on the path.

As you move through the course, I invite you to expand time. Though it may only take you a couple of hours to complete, when you slow down and savor those moments, you may discover what took me years to learn:

Love itself has been holding you all along.

The Path is trustworthy.

And you're ready now, not because you've "arrived," but because transformation happens as you walk.

You can visit *awakencoachinstitute.com/ the-awaken-way* to begin.

In the Great Love, **Christi**

ACKNOWLEDGEMENTS

Thanks first to the spirit of unconditional love that runs through us all. It's been so powerful to feel connected as humans to so many, because we're all part of The Great Love.

And to my parents, who gave me life and instilled in me the value of respect for every human across cultures. This gift of being human is miraculous—I can't even believe some days how incredible it is to see, hear, and feel all the beauty in the world.

Tara Westover, in her book *Educated*, asks, "How much of ourselves should we give to those we love? And how much must we betray them to grow up?" I wonder if it has been a betrayal to tell the truth as I experienced it, even if my memories are different from those of others. Even if I was the villain in their story. It's okay to stop betraying myself and start believing myself, not as a victim or a hero, but as the author of my life. I'm grateful to all the authors before me who wrote their stories and have given me the courage to write mine.

And thanks to my nearest and dearest:

Ben, you are the love of my life. You've stuck with me since we first met when I was running from home at age 16. You've seen and loved all parts of me, and we've been growing up together all this time. Our teenage selves arranged quite the marriage. I know being married to someone with such a high ACE (Adverse Childhood Experiences) score is difficult, and your patience is priceless to me.

Sometimes when my women friends describe what they'd love in a partner, they describe a man who's tender and warm, thoughtful and attentive, in touch with his emotions, and also takes full responsibility at home. Whenever I hear those descriptions, I'm reminded how lucky I am to be with someone like you daily. You're a daily kind of guy.

I know you would not want to be put on a pedestal, like I sometimes do. Thanks for allowing me access to the parts of you that get anxious, lonely, melancholy, and contemplative, and for sharing your story of growing up "other," too. You've been on your own journey, right alongside me.

Micah Byerly, our eldest child and a dear friend. You have gently taught me how to be kind, honest, and to speak from firm, loving boundaries. From your first day, you've communicated your needs and wants loudly, gently, and clearly. Your fun and warmth make your stubborn streak all the more lovely. Micah, I find you astounding.

Leila Byerly, the family member I feel most similar to, and the one who challenges me to love more fiercely. You have the incredible ability to apologize, to take responsibility for your own actions, and to speak the truth. Plus, you're a ton of fun and a fabulous travel companion. I love you, Lele.

Raven Byerly, our newest grown-up member. It's a pleasure seeing you stepping into adulthood with kindness, consideration, helpfulness, and willingness to learn. Keep being exactly yourself—your presence in the world is a delight. I'm so grateful you're part of our family.

And to my darling sister Kathryn. You have known me since the day you were born and have loved me with the fiercest, tender love. I'm so glad we have an adult friendship with so much understanding for one another and freedom to make our choices without fear of disappointment. Your courage and power continue to inspire me.

Thanks to my many soulmates in the helping professions, and the Awaken Coaches Community. These years growing together with hundreds of people willing to do the brave and challenging soul-work of loving ourselves more deeply has been the honor of my life. You are too numerous to name, but I'm holding each of you dearly in my heart. My special thanks go to:

Sister Pat Smith, thank you for teaching me that experiencing being loved is the heart of all true spirituality. And for your years of patience, which is one of the hallmarks of true love.

My Aunt Vicki Joy, thank you for loving yourself, your husband, your five children, and numerous grandchildren wholeheartedly, and for modeling what it is to allow others to be who they are, without attempting to be god for them.

To my Beloved Community sisters: Grace Remington, Michelle Wiegers, Jill Pratt, and Megan McDonald—you know what you mean to me on this Camino journey. Thank you for your consistent love, your vast wells of creativity, and for being the authors of your lives along with me.

Joan Leteipa, thanks for letting me take over your home for ten days as I dove into the writing. Even as I sat in your beautiful ocean-side home, you showed me constant love and affection and lived this verse: 1 John 4:18-19 Such love has no fear, because perfect love expels all fear.

Valeyne Grotrian, thank you for decades of soul friendship, made deeper by our mutual journeys toward trusting our inner wisdom and living in the fullness of life.

Stacy Crawford, your wisdom and openness have been a source of strength for me. I love watching you live your life fearlessly and appreciate your regular love notes.

Basia Goodwin, your sacred rituals and your loving warmth are gifts. The way you hold dark and light, dusk and dawn, for me and for Awaken each year at Flores del Camino is magical. It's what I most look forward to all year round.

Ellany Lea, for gently and lovingly inviting business badassery, and making Awaken possible. I hope all over-achievers everywhere follow aaaaaaaaaall your advice.

Kerri Garner, for letting me know that I'm likable enough that someone would want to spend time with me, and for teaching me to swear.

Molly Davis Moon, for helping me find the boundaries that were always inside. Maaaaan, does it make everything easier.

And of course, Amy Warren, my editor and partner in this effort. Your gentleness, structure, adaptability and continual reassurances that my stories are "not cringy at all" provided the container to keep telling them.

ABOUT THE AUTHOR

C hristi Byerly, MCC is the founder of Awaken Coach Institute. She lives in Alsace, France with her husband Ben, two cats, and lots of plants. She is delighted when her three adult children visit.

After moving away from the punitive evangelical system she was raised in, Christi discovered what she now teaches: Love itself is the foundation, the Path is trustworthy, and transformation happens in the midst of the mess.

For over a decade, she has trained hundreds of coaches. Through Awaken's ICF-accredited programs, she is building communities of grace—places where people learn to trust Love as the source rather than their own performance.

Christi's coaching process motivates people to create communities of empathy and grace around them and to live their mission as part of something bigger than themselves.

Holy Rebellion is her first book.